Exploring Web 2.0:

Second Generation Internet Tools -

Blogs, Podcasts, Wikis, Networking, Virtual Worlds, and More

By

Ann Bell

Katy Crossing Press

Exploring Web 2.0: Second Generation Interactive Tools –

Blogs, Podcasts, Wikis, Networking, Virtual Worlds, and More

Front cover photo compliments of iStockphoto.com

Katy Crossing Press
300 Katy Crossing
Georgetown, TX 78626

ISBN: 1-4414-4986-8
ISBN-13: 978-1-4414-4986-3

Ann Bell can be reached at annamaebell@yahoo.com

Additional resources and information can be found at
http://www.annamaebell.com

PDF Online®
pbwiki®
Photoworks®
PodSafe Music
Network®
Popfly®
ProQuest®
QuickTime®
Radio Shack®
Read/Write/Think
Timeline ®
Recording Industry
Association of
America (RIAA) ®
RockYou®
Safari®
SamePoint.com®
SchoolTube®

SecondLife®
Shelfari®
Shutterfly®
SimCity®
SkyDrive®
Skype®
Slide®
Slideroll™
Snapfish®
STOCK-TRAK®
SurveyMonkey®
Tapped In®
TeacherTube®
Technorati®
TechSmith®
ThinkFree®
Thinkquest®
Twitter®

TypePad®
UnitedStreaming®
UNIX®
Vlog It®
VoiceThread®
Vox®
Weekly Reader®
Whyville®
Wikibooks®
Wikipedia®
WikiSpaces®
Windows®
WordPress®
Xanga®
Xtimeline®
Yahoo! ®
YouTube®
Zamzar®

Readers should contact the appropriate companies for more complete information regarding trademarks and registration.

TABLE OF CONTENTS

TABLE OF FIGURES

About the Author

Ann Bell is an Adjunct Online Professional Development Instructor and Course Developer for the University of Wisconsin-Stout. She has developed and instructs the courses *Digital Media and Visual Literacy, Learning Applications for the iPod® and Handheld Computers,* and *Implementing Instructional Technology Innovations.* Mrs. Bell has been a high school media specialist for twenty years in Iowa, Montana, Oregon, and Guam.

Ann received her B.A. degree from the University of Northern Iowa, a library media endorsement from the University of Montana, and a Master of Library and Information Studies from the University of Hawaii. She has completed postgraduate work at Drake University and the University of Northern Iowa.

Ann was the recipient of the 2001 Information Technology Pathfinder Award from the American Association of School Librarians and the Follett Software Company and the 2002 recipient of the Iowa Educational Media Association Lamplighter Award.

Ann has published two books for Linworth Publishing, Inc., *Creating Digital Video in Your School: How to Shoot, Edit Produce, Distribute and Incorporate Digital Media into the Curriculum* and *Handheld Computers in Schools and Media Centers,* nine novels for Heartsong Presents, and two novels for Barbour Publishing. Gale-Thorndike Press released this same series in a large print edition.

Mrs. Bell was selected to be included in the *2008 Contemporary Authors (volume 259)* series by the Thomson Gale Publishers.

INTRODUCTION

In recent months, exciting changes began happening on the World Wide Web. More services and features were becoming available, but most Internet users were unaware of this new potential until the 'Net Generation' began embracing the new Web-based tools in a way that often confounded other generations. While their parents and teachers were passive consumers of media, youth today became active creators of media content and hungry for interaction. (Tapscott 46)

Pew Internet and American Life Project's survey of U.S. teenagers confirms that more than half (some 57 percent) of online teens are what the project calls "content creators." (Tapscott 52) Skills the Net Generation are using at their first jobs are often not ones that they have learned within the school system, but ones that have been self-taught from online resources or peers. Older generations are often mystified with what is a way of life for those born after 1990. The less technology savvy users, or those with limited resources, are finding themselves falling further behind in the job market and with personal communication than those taking advantage of the latest resources available online.

Many parents and employers believe that schools are failing to prepare their students for worthwhile careers in the 21st century. At the same time, schools feel overwhelmed by the lack of funding, additional professional training needed for their teachers, and the responsibility of protecting the safety and privacy of their students.

After much research on the differences in what students were experiencing after 4:00 p.m. and what was happening in their lives before 4:00 p.m., it became apparent that educators needed a reference guide to broaden their instructional tools arsenal to help them meet this increasing need in preparing students for the 21st century workforce. *Exploring Web 2.0: Second Generation Interactive Tools – Blogs, Podcasts, Wikis, Networking, Virtual Worlds, and More* is designed to help the casual computer user, students, parents, and teachers understand the latest in free or inexpensive web tools and its power for research, collaboration, and communication. What is becoming commonplace in the business world needs to be embraced by the educational community for both learning and personal use. The established worker in the business world needs to become comfortable to the online tools and experiences that the younger workers bring to the workforce.

Exploring Web 2.0 contains a detailed index, a glossary, and Works Cited. Links to additional resources will be incorporated into each chapter and topic so that readers can further research the topic. Chapter 1 provides the history, background, and current overview of Web 2.0. It will demystify the current jargon connected with this latest web phenomenon.

Chapter 2 provides the background and uses of RSS feeds, the main building block of Web 2.0. Chapter 3 continues by exploring the use of metadata, tags, tag clouds, and folksonomy, which are the strength of this latest technology. Chapter 4 applies tags, tag clouds, and metadata to *online* bookmarks while chapter five applies them to *online* photo libraries.

Chapters 6, 7, and 8 cover the use of blogs, podcasts, vodcasts, and screencasts on the web. The same underlying technology applies to each of these online formats except one is based primarily on text, one on audio, and the others on video.

Chapter 9 covers the strengths of utilizing and developing wikis as a collaboration tool. Chapter 10 covers the development and uses of Mash-ups for educational and informational purposes. Using mash-ups stimulate creativity as they combine data from a variety of sources to create an entirely different program.

Chapter 11 explores the development and advantages of using a *Virtual Office* and online storage space. Chapter 12 explores the possibilities of e-learning course management systems and a variety of online training tools. A special emphasis is placed on Moodle, a free, Open Source software package designed to help educators create effective online learning communities.

Chapter 13 provides the background and development of social networking, its impact on sharing news and information to a schools' community, as well as using online social networking for career development.

Chapter 14 delves into the background and development of SecondLife and other interactive sites. These multi-user environments can be incorporated into the curriculum, used for personal training, as well as being utilized within the business community.

Chapter 15 introduces the reader to the multiple communications features of Web 2.0. A simple computer microphone and webcam are becoming vital hardware tools for online corporate meetings, group collaboration, or personal communications.

Exploring Web 2.0: Second Generation Interactive Tools can be read from beginning to end to obtain an overview of the online Web 2.0 resources that are available or it can be used as a reference tool to consult when investigating and utilizing individual Web 2.0 tools.

Chapter 1

Exploring Web 2.0

WHAT IS WEB 2.0?

A silent revolution is overtaking the Internet and affecting how business people, educators, and students research, collaborate, communicate, and retrieve information. This revolution has been nicknamed Web 2.0 (pronounced "Web two point Oh".)

What constitutes Web 2.0 has been the center of controversy for some time. Is this an entirely new era, or merely the continual evolution of the World Wide Web of the 1990s? Ultimately, the label "Web 2.0" is far less important than the concepts, projects, and practices included in its scope. (Alexander 33) Regardless of a person's viewpoint concerning Web 2.0, almost everyone agrees something new and different is happening. Business people, students, and teachers are beginning to use the Internet differently. The Web is being seen as a programming platform that allows casual computer users to create software applications of their own.

The read-only of Web 1.0 of yesterday was based on an *information silo* premise. This means the early resources on the World Wide Web could not exchange information with other related systems within its own organization; all data was self-contained. The "publish and browse" format of most Web sites left most users as readers and consumers, since complex coding was involved in its development. However, all this changed when the Publish/Browse format gave way to a Read/Write format of Web 2.0. The knowledge, resources, and computing power of billions of people are now coming together into a massive collective force.

Many argue that the bursting of the dot-com bubble in the fall of 2001 marked a turning point for the web. At that time, countless people concluded that the web was over-hyped, when in reality it marked the turning point for the web. The concept of "Web 2.0" began with a conference brainstorming session with Tim O'Reilly and MediaLive International in 2004 (O'Reilly).

The phrase *Web 2.0* came to refer to a perceived second generation of web-based communities and hosted services aimed to facilitate collaboration and sharing between users. Using these newer applications, the Web itself acts as the computer; services once limited to computer desktops are now available online.

An appealing feature of the development of Web 2.0 applications is that many of its services are based on the OpenSource format in which anyone with programming skills can use, modify, or remix a program with a completely separate, independent one. This OpenSource concept makes the program free or inexpensive, and by using Web 2.0 tools, users no longer need to be concerned about expensive licensing agreements. Web users who do not have programming skills can use their online creations, plus take advantage of their shared expertise.

In Web 2.0 applications, the viewable content is not as likely to be in the print-page style. Rather than viewing the

Web as a book, it is now being viewed as *microcontent*. Blogs are about posts, not pages. Wikis are streams of conversation, revision, amendment, and truncation. The *content* blocks can be saved, summarized, addressed, copied, quoted, and built into new projects. (Alexander 33)

Probably the creator of the name and pioneer in the field, Tim O'Reilly, gives the best definition of Web 2.0.

> "Web 2.0 is the network as platform, spanning all connected devices; Web 2.0 applications are those that make the most of the intrinsic advantages of that platform: delivering software as a continually updated service that gets better the more people use it, consuming and remixing data from multiple sources, including individual users, while providing their own data and services in a form that allows remixing by others, creating network effects through an "architecture of participation," and going beyond the page metaphor of Web 1.0 to deliver rich user experiences."
> (http://radar.oreilly.com/archives/2005/10/web_20_compact_d efinition.html)

Many have tried to explain and simplify the uniqueness of these web applications. Dion Hinchcliffe helps to clarify their uniqueness in his blog of April 2, 2006 when he describes the Key Aspects of Web 2.0 as:

- the Web and all its connected devices as one global platform of reusable services and data
- data consumption and remixing from all sources, particularly user generated data
- continuous and seamless update of software and data, often very rapidly

- rich and interactive user interfaces
- architecture of participation that encourages user contribution (State of Web 2.0)

The acceptance of these new technologies, services, and tools for the World Wide Web reached a turning point when at the end of 2006, Time magazine's Person of the Year was 'You'. On the cover of the magazine, underneath the title of the award, was a picture of a PC with a mirror in place of the screen, reflecting not only the face of the reader, but also the general feeling that 2006 was the year of the Web - a new, improved, 'second version', 'user generated' Web. (Anderson 4)

SERVICES INVOLVED IN WEB 2.0

Web 2.0 is about data first, experiences and functionality lag far behind in second place. Whether it is text, images, audio, or video, the Web ultimately revolves around data. You cannot have presentation without something to present. However, that data is of little value unless the teacher or student arranges it into a meaningful presentation.

The development of Web 2.0 brings together three parallel streams of development.

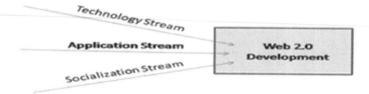

Figure -1:1 Web 2.0 Development

1. The technology stream provides the underlying infrastructure groundwork of networking and hardware technology and software. This stream includes service-oriented architectures (SOA) such as Feeds, RSS, Web Services, and Mashups.

2. The applications stream includes Rich Internet Applications (RIA), which are desktop-like services and applications that are used on the Internet. These applications lead to seamless navigation, without interruptions of one's activity. Over the coming years, it will be increasingly rare to buy software for installation on a local machine. Instead, almost all software will be delivered as a service through the web, and these same applications will often provide components that can be used seamlessly in other applications.

3. The socialization stream includes user participation and contribution on the Web. The social web includes tagging, Wikis, podcasting, vodcasting, and blogging.

Each of these streams and applications of development will be discussed in detail in later chapters.

IMPACT OF WEB 2.0

How will Web 2.0 affect you as a parent, teacher, student, businessperson, or casual user? The new trends on the Internet probably already affect you, without you realizing it. You are able to navigate easier and find matching results for your search queries appropriate for your context with more precision. You may be using Web sites just as you use desktop applications: seamless navigation, without interruptions of your activity. You may have customized your user interfaces on your favorite search engine according to your preferences and needs. It is now easier to communicate with colleagues, professional organizations, friends, and partners to share ideas, media, and information. You may be receiving instant news updates. You may also be putting your knowledge to use, by co-authoring content on encyclopedias and wikis since the development strategy is shifting from coding everything from scratch (re-inventing the wheel) to assembling ready-made components (making a better wheel) (Adobe).

Not to step up and maximize Web 2.0 resources for teaching, learning and driving innovation is to risk becoming marginalized as a viable influence in helping to share the 21st century.

SPEED OF READING INCREASED

Another change that affects how a person uses the Internet is that the speed of reading in the digital age is changing. Internet users must learn to adapt and modify their reading styles according to the appropriate situation. Being able to *surf* countless Web pages, scanning information, might be a good practice for cursory knowledge acquisition, but it does not lend itself to in-depth reading. In fact, these are almost two separate mental practices.

It is important to learn to distinguish between skimming for information and in-depth reading. Reading on the Internet requires both skills. The first for a quick analysis to find what is worth reading, using keywords and sub-headings to determine the relevancy of the Web page. The second style of reading is a slow analysis to consider the importance of the information that has been retrieved.

RSS news feeds allow users to determine what is worth reading in depth and what is not. They provide a way to receive content in short summaries, easy to scan so the user can select what they want to read.

DEVELOP HIGHER ORDER THINKING SKILLS

Developing higher-order thinking skills is not an easy task. Historically, educators have looked to Bloom's Taxonomy (1956) for assistance. Bloom's model divided thinking skills into lower-order and higher-order knowledge. During the 1990's a new group of cognitive psychologists, led by Lorin Anderson (a former student of Bloom's), updated the taxonomy reflecting relevance to 21st century work.

The use of Web 2.0 applications can be excellent instructional tools to assist learners in moving up the ladder toward higher-order thinking skills from remembering, to understanding, to applying, to analyzing, to evaluating, to finally creating, the ultimate strength and purpose of the newer applications.

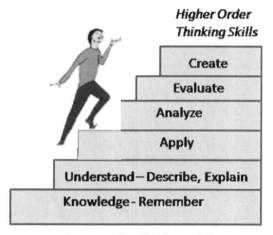

Figure 1:2 Bloom's Taxonomy

INCREASED PARTICIPATION AND CREATIVITY

The new Web services permit users to increase their emphasis on participation and creativity, and allow them to reach out to new audiences. Interactivity is a chief feature of most new online tools while existing digital resources are presented more efficiently.

CURRENT RETRIEVAL UPDATED

One of the changes on the web is that blogs, most social bookmarking tools, and other Web 2.0 services are organized in reverse chronological order. Their very architecture orients them, or at least their front pages, toward the present moment. Given bloggers' inclination for linking, not to mention some services' ability to search links, blogs, and other platforms readily lead the searcher to further sources. Users can search the blogosphere for political commentary, current cultural items, public developments in science, business news like never before. (Alexander 40)

KEEPING STUDENTS SAFE

The biggest concern of parents and schools today is keeping the students in a safe environment, both physically and digitally. One of the most difficult roads to navigate in the world of the Read/Write Web is balancing the safety of the child with the benefits that come with students researching online and taking ownership of the work they publish online.

In the digital world, Internet safety is more than not publishing children's names and pictures on the Internet or permitting students to access obscene content online. These are acts the federal and state laws regulate and all schools do their best to enforce. Safety is also about responsibility, appropriateness, and common sense, as well. If we ask our students to publish as part of a class assignment, or if we know they are publishing outside of the classroom (which they are), it is our obligation to teach them what is acceptable and safe and what is not. (Richardson 10)

Many schools filter Web 2.0 sites without understanding the value and potential of many of these sites for educational purposes. Schools will need to evaluate each site on case-by-case basis and individually unblock those sites that educators would be able to use to strengthen their particular curriculum area. Those decisions are judgment calls based on the maturity of the students and the value of the site.

In making these difficult decisions we first need to decide who the audience is. Is it just a small peer group? The whole class? The entire Internet? In nearly all Web 2.0 applications, there are ways to set usage privileges of the intended audience. Care needs to be taken to set the correct parameters when an activity is first set up on the Web to avoid unexpected privacy issues.

We need to educate our children and youth about privacy, trust, and the World Wide Web. Those who participate in the social networks of Web 2.0 applications often do not appreciate the reach of that network. Posting on an open social network means that millions of people could potentially view their profile with long-term implications for what is displayed.

SUMMARY

The digital world is rapidly changing around us. Users are challenged not only to be aware of those changes, but also to take advantage of the new resources to best meet their information, communication, and collaborative needs.

Since student safety is of paramount concern for educators, parents, and law-enforcement officers, society as a whole cannot ignore the rapid changes that are taking place on the Internet. Its mastery is vital for the 21st century workforce. The best way to protect young people is to teach them the strengths and weaknesses of Web 2.0 resources.

Applying Web 2.0 resources improve users' higher order thinking skills. They improve users' creativity and ability to collaborate with peers, which is essential for the 21st century workforce. If parents, educators, and the current workforce, do not keep pace with the technology that young people use on a daily basis, they risk becoming irrelevant and will have little or no impact on the future of society as a whole.

Chapter 2

RSS FEEDS

WHAT ARE RSS FEEDS?

RSS feeds organize content that is updated on a regular basis so that others can retrieve it with ease in a systematic manner. This content could be articles, blog posts, photos, PDF documents, PowerPoint Presentations, audio files, video files or other applications.

RSS is an acronym that stands for Rich Site Summary or Really Simple Syndication. Really Simple Syndication (RSS) is a lightweight XML format designed for sharing headlines and other Web content. Most people are interested in many Web sites whose content changes on an unpredictable schedule. Repeatedly checking each Web site to see if there is any new content can be very tedious and time consuming.

> RSS – **R**eally **S**imple **S**yndication or **R**ich **S**ite **S**ummary

RSS works by having the Web site author maintain a list of notifications on their site. This list of notifications is called an *RSS Feed*. RSS uses very basic information to prepare its notification. Each list of items is presented in order from the most recent to oldest. Each item usually consists of a simple title describing the item along with a more complete description and a link to a Web page with the actual information being described.

RSS allows web authors to easily syndicate (or publish) their content online for others to use. These RSS feeds allow the syndication of lists of hyperlinks, along with other information, or *metadata*. This syndication is an easy way to distribute a list of headlines, update notices and sometimes content to a wide number of people. The additional information helps viewers decide whether they want to follow the link. Each metadata contains a title, summary, and a link to a URL. Other information, such as the date, creator's name, etc., may also be available within the RSS feed.

RSS Aggregators: Software or a hosted application that collects RSS feeds from various sources and displays it in a single consolidated view, either in a window on your desktop or in a Web browser.

Educators who are interested in finding out the latest headlines or changes can subscribe to this list. Special computer programs called "RSS aggregators" automatically access the RSS feeds of preselected Web sites and organize the results for the user. (RSS feeds and aggregators are sometimes called "RSS Channels" and "RSS Readers.")

Of the three types of feeds commonly found on Web sites, RSS 1.0, RSS 2.0 and Atom, there is a great deal of debate as to which one is the best XML format. For simplicity, most people will refer to all feeds simply as RSS.

Feeds are most commonly referred to as pulling, rather than a pushing technology. Pushing technology is broadcasting a message and hoping that someone will come by your Web site or your television station to listen or view to it. RSS is pulling technology because visitors subscribe to your message and can retrieve it whenever they want. This is a shift toward a "just in time" approach to information and concept understanding. The benefit of this type of technology is the user's ability to select (subscribe to) a particular RSS feed and then have the content updated in real time.

WHY USE RSS FEEDS?

Many people are interested in Web sites such as news sites, community and religious organization information pages, product update pages, medical Web sites, and weblogs whose content changes on an unpredictable schedule. Before RSS Feeds were available, users would have to go to each page, load it, remember how it is formatted, and find where they last left off in the list.

E-mail notification of changes was an early solution to this problem. Unfortunately, when you receive email notifications from multiple Web sites they are usually disorganized and can get overwhelming, and are often mistaken for spam. RSS is a better way to be notified of new and changed content. Notifications of changes to multiple Web sites are handled easily, and the results are presented to you well -organized and distinct from email.

The feed your aggregator checks is virus free and you know that everything in your aggregator is something you want to read because you chose to subscribe to it. There are no ads, no spam; just new content from the sources you want to read. You can scan the headlines, read the entire post, click through to the actual Web site, and file the information away for later retrieval.

Another feature of RSS is that it contains only the content from Web sites; it removes the eye candy that encompasses many Web pages today. A nice feature of some aggregator is the ability to create your own template and pull the Web site content from your feeds into it. This is often called Web content customizability. You can see how this is literally changing the face of the World Wide Web. (D'Souza 15)

HOW TO UTILIZE RSS FEEDS

If you view an RSS file in a web browser most of the time you will see raw XML text and not a formatted Web page as you do in HTML.

```
<?xml version="1.0" encoding="UTF-8" ?>
<rss version="2.0" xml:lang="en" xmlns:content="http://purl.org/rss/1.0/modules/content/" xmlns:itunes="http://www.itunes.com/dtds/podcast-1.0.dtd"
xmlns:dc="http://purl.org/dc/elements/1.1/" >
  <channel>
      <title>Educational Technology Resources</title>
      <link>http://www.annamaebell.com/</link>
      <description>Tips and Resources for the use of educational technology in the K-12 classroom.</description>
      <itunes:summary>Tips and Resources for the use of educational technology in the K-12 classroom.</itunes:summary>
<dc:subject>Education K-12</dc:subject>
      <itunes:category text="Education">
      <itunes:category text="K-12"/>
      </itunes:category>
      <language>en</language>
<dc:rights>Copyright 2007</dc:rights>
      <itunes:author>Ann Bell</itunes:author>
      <itunes:owner>
          <itunes:name>Ann Bell</itunes:name>
          <itunes:email>annamaebell@yahoo.com</itunes:email>
      </itunes:owner>
      <itunes:explicit>no</itunes:explicit>
      <managingEditor>annamaebell@yahoo.com (Ann Bell)</managingEditor>
<webMaster>annamaebell@yahoo.com</webMaster>
          <image><url>http://www.annamaebell.com/images/student_mediaplayer2.jpg</url><title>Educational Technology
Resources</title><link>http://www.annamaebell.com/</link></image>
      <lastBuildDate>Thu, 23 Aug 2007 23:52:46 GMT</lastBuildDate>
      <pubDate>Thu, 23 Aug 2007 23:52:46 GMT</pubDate>
      <generator>RSS DreamFeeder v 2.1.0</generator>
```

Figure 2:1 – RSS Raw Text

To view an RSS feed properly, you need to subscribe to a type of software called an *aggregator* or feed collector that checks the feeds you subscribe to, usually every hour, and collects all the new content from those sites. When you are ready, you simply open your aggregator to read the individual stories, file them for later use, click through to the site itself, or delete them. (Richards 76)

In order to subscribe to an RSS newsfeed you will need two things, an RSS reader (also known as a news aggregator) and the URL (web address) of the RSS feed that you wish to subscribe.

To sign up for an RSS feed simply open a Web site and look for an orange and white striped icon in the search engine toolbar (usually next to the Home icon), which means that RSS feed capability is available for this page. If there is no RSS feed for this page, the icon will be gray and white. Follow the instructions for your particular newsreader to subscribe.

Figure 2:2 – RSS Icons

When subscribing to a feed, you do not disclose your e-mail address, so you do not increase your exposure to threats associated with e-mail: spam, viruses, phishing and identity theft. If you want to stop receiving news, you do not have to send an "unsubscribe" request like what is common with most Listserv. If you want to be removed from a particular RSS Feed, you simply remove the feed from your aggregator. The feed items are automatically *sorted* in the sense that each feed URL has its own sets of entries (unlike an e-mail box, where all mails are in one big pile and e-mail programs have to re-sort according to complicated rules and pattern matching) The major search engines such as My Yahoo! (http://my.yahoo.com/), Google Reader (http://www.google.com/reader/), msn.com (http://my.msn.com/) contain RSS feed aggregators. In addition, many web browsers such as Safari, Firefox, and Internet Explorer 7.0 allow receipts of feeds from the tool bar using *Live Bookmarks, Favorites,* and other techniques to integrate feed reading into a browser.

Other feed readers include:

- Bloglines (http://www.bloglines.com/)
- NewsGator (http://www.newsgator.com/)
- SharpReader (http://www.sharpreader.net/)
- NetNewsWire (http://www.newsgator.com/NetNewsWire.aspx) for the MAC

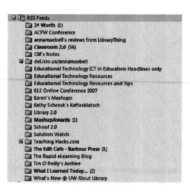

Many e-mail applications may also provide a way of reading feeds. Outlook 2007 contains a feed reader and checks for RSS feeds at the same time it checks for new e-mail.

Online web applications like Phone Feeds

Figure 2:3 – Outlook RSS Aggregator

(http://www.phonefeeds.com/), My Yahoo! Mobile RSS (http://mobile.yahoo.com/) and Lite Feeds (http://www.litefeeds.com/) make it easy to reformat RSS feeds for use in mobile devices like a PDA, Blackberry or mobile phone.

CREATING AN RSS FEED

If you have a Web site, blog, podcast, vodcasts, or other online postings that you would like to attract more users you will want to create an RSS Feed to 'pull' users to your site. This is done by creating an XML file. To save you the headache of having to hand code an RSS feed, there are a number of free or inexpensive *Feed Generators* available. (See Appendix B) An example of such a Feed Generator is FeedForAll (http://www.feedforall.com/), an easy to use software application that formats the XML for you.

If you build your Web site with Dreamweaver, and spend a great deal of time updating pages and posting content, you may want to get your content republished in portals and news sites like Yahoo and Google News. This can be done by using the RSS Feed generator known as DreamFeeder (http://www.rnsoft.com/en/products/rssdreamfeeder/.) This program lets you prepare your RSS feeds from within Dreamweaver without retyping your content and without having to know any new RSS/XML codes.

RSS feeds contain what are referred to as "items." The items (generally Web pages that you would like others to link to) are usually connected in some way and contain a common theme or other similarity. To enter your item into the RSS file, you will need three bits of information: title, description, and link.

USES OF RSS FEEDS IN EDUCATION

Many teachers and library media specialists like to customize the Front (start) page on their classroom or lab computers using RSS Feeds. Students would then see the aggregated subject specific resources, bookmarks, and other content whenever they logon. My Yahoo!, Google Reader, msn.com and other services contain the capabilities of adding RSS Feeds to their start pages.

Another popular use of RSS Feed in schools is to have students share their feed lists based upon specific topics or on a subject area. These feeds could include search queries, blogs, research, and other informational feeds. By sharing RSS Feeds, students are able to share information and save time on their collaboration projects.

Many schools, universities, and businesses are realizing that RSS feeds can be an effective tool for disseminating information. A common use is to use programs that display multiple RSS feeds in a single interface that can be incorporated into a Web page. This allows users to see announcements, news and product information from several Web sites at one time.

ProQuest is one of the first periodical databases that included aggregators to utilize RSS feeds. This is an easy way for students and educators to create valuable, in-context links to their ProQuest subscription content. Users can be notified when articles meeting designated keyword descriptions are added to the database.

"RSS enclosures can make it really easy for teachers to distribute files to their students. A teacher could post lecture notes, multimedia content, or any other kind of electronic document and let each student's RSS Reader take care of the rest. Similarly, school principals could use RSS to distribute newsletters or other materials to parents who are subscribed to a school's news feed." (Using RSS)

If teachers already use Weblogs, they are beginning to see the potential of RSS Feeds. Instead of checking all 25 (or 30, or more) student Weblogs every day, they can simply collect their work in their aggregator using their RSS feeds. That way, they can scan through all of the class content in one place, make sure it is all appropriate, and click through to a particular post if they want to comment on it. This method drastically reduces reading time and allows educators to move their classes closer to becoming paperless.

In addition, teachers can provide individual student Weblog feeds to parents, counselors, or whoever might be interested in that student's work and are savvy enough to know about RSS feeds. With some Weblog packages, you can even subscribe to feeds that show new comments on the various sites, or even to just certain topics. In other words, you can track about everything going on in your student blogs using RSS feeds.

Even if students do not have Weblogs, you may want to have them set up their own Bloglines or other Feed Aggregator account. With more and more news sources producing feeds for aggregation, the breadth of current events and even topic-specific research that students could collect could go a long way to assisting them with research and further study.

The idea of aggregating research feeds is becoming extremely common. For example, if a student is doing a project or a paper on global warming, they could create an RSS feed that would bring any news about global warming to his aggregator as soon as it was published.

Students can create a feed about any topic they choose. If they want to create a feed for what is in the daily news about a particular topic, they can syndicate any Google News section or any search you do on Google News. To create a feed for a section on their page, they merely need to click on the section they are interested, and then click on the "RSS" or "Atom" link on the left side of the page. For instance, if they click on the "RSS" link while on the Business page, they will get an RSS feed for business news.

If new content about global warming is added to a site that is already on the Internet, or if there is an entirely new site created about the topic, they can find out about it in their aggregator. This is done by going to Googlealerts.com and signing up for a free account. Once they are registered, they can create up to five searches that can bring back up to 150 results total. They merely need to fill in the form with the search terms they want, click "Run Searches Automatically," and click "Update." When they are finished, they merely click the link in the left hand column

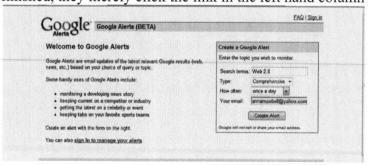

Figure 2:4 Google

where it says "Feed Settings." All of their searches will
come up, and they can check the box that says "RSS Feed"
next to each one of the searches.

Another way to get continually updated news about various
topics with RSS Feeds is to use the feeds provided by
Moreover.com. This site provides a large list of predefined
topic searches at
(http://w.moreover.com/categories/category_list_rss.html).
You can find even more of these types of Moreover feeds
(including ones for your favorite sports teams, the state you
live in or your favorite interest level) on the Syndic8.com
site
(http://www.syndic8.com/feedcat.php?Scheme=Syndic8).

Most traditional news outlets provide RSS Feeds of their
content. To find out if your favorite publication has an RSS
feed, do a Google search with the publication name and
"RSS" and see what comes up.

SUMMARY

As information on the Internet multiplied, users became
overwhelmed with having to go to each Web site to search
for updates. This problem was solved with the development
of RSS Feeds, which gather all the feeds that the user
subscribed into one organized place. At the user's
convenience, he can simply open his aggregator and read
the individual stories, file them for later use, click through
to the site itself, or delete them.

Soon after new technologies appeared on the Web,
educators began applying them not only for their personal
use but also for their professional development. With a
little creativity, teachers began using RSS Feeds with their
students to meet both technology standards and content

area standards to prepare them with information and communications skills for the 21st century. However, much needs to be done to make these valuable resources available to students at all levels.

Chapter 3

METADATA, TAGS, TAG CLOUDS, AND FOLKSONOMY

DESCRIPTION
Like RSS, metadata, tagging and folksonomies are a major part of the transformation to the Read/Write Web. Tagging harnesses a technology called XML to allow users to affix descriptive labels or keywords to content (techies call them *metadata*, or data about data.) (Tapscott 41)

> **Folksonomy** - The method of collaboratively creating and managing tags to annotate and categorize content.

Generally, three classes of metadata can be differentiated:

1. professionally created metadata, typically a catalog compiled by a group of professionals,
2. author-created metadata that refers to people describing self-created documents
3. user-created metadata assigned by any user of a document and typically shared throughout a community. (Vossen 201)

HISTORY OF TAGGING AND FOLKSONOMY

The history of tagging is a much older topic than most realize. One of the first consumer products to include tagging or annotations was the Lotus Magellan product, which appeared in 1988 and allowed annotations of documents and objects on one's hard drive to ease finding and re-finding them. By the mid-90s, CompuServe included tagging for objects uploaded into its forum libraries. In 2001, Bitzi allowed tagging of any media that had a URL.

Search engines before Google relied on author-prepared meta-tags on HTML pages to catalog, or categorize a given page. These meta-tags were hidden from the visible page, but helped define data on the page. In theory, this sounded good. In practice, the hidden meta-tags were often used in ways they were never intended, including the addition of excessive or irrelevant keywords. On-purpose manipulation of these tags was used to obtain higher ranks in search results.

TAGS

User-generated tags differ from traditional subject indexing metadata in that they are not generated by experts but by creators and consumers of the content. User-generated tags are easier and more flexible than fitting information into

Tag - a user-generated keyword or term assigned for the purpose of keyword-based classification and search of information.

preconceived categories or folders.

Users can assign as many tags to a web file as he desires and then rename or delete that tag later. Usually tags are freely chosen keywords and are used instead of a controlled vocabulary of a traditional taxonomy such as Sears Subject Headings.

There are two types of tags: *organizational* and *social*. Organizational tags can be subdivided into a personal and an intrapersonal form of organization. Using organizational tags, users can sort and find their own items, retrieve them in the future, share them with others, as well as use another person's scheme of organization. Social tags are designed to benefit an entire community of users.

A tag cloud is a visual depiction of content tags used on digital media. In the graphic format, the more frequently used tags are displayed in a larger font. In the ordered format, the displayed list is generally alphabetical. Selecting a single tag within a tag cloud will generally lead to a collection of items that are associated with that tag word. You will need time to explore tag clouds since there are often too many tags in use that a full presented at one time. Tag clouds allow a user

Tag Cloud of President Barak Obama's Inauguration Speech
Figure 3:1 Tag Cloud

to group their available resources as well as find the unexpected. Thus, intuitive ways to explore the tag clouds enable serendipitous discoveries.

The premise behind tag clouds is that the users know best. Their actions determine how other users navigate. Their choices leave a trail. Typically, though not always, the "important," the more heavily used, topics get bigger while those considered less important, or the less popular ones, get smaller. Once they get small enough, they disappear. Instead of a hierarchy based on user-centered classification systems, the tag cloud "hierarchy" is based on raw usage. The main problem with tag clouds is that either the topic gains immediate, widespread traction with the public or it disappears from the cloud. Once it disappears, it is as if it never existed. Few users will ever find that particular tag again.

FOLKSONOMY

Thomas Vander Wal coined the term Folksonomy in 2005 by combining the words *taxonomy* and *folk,* thereby expressing the impact of people (folks) on classification (the Greek word *taxis* that stands for classification) and management (the Greek word *nomia* means management). *Folksonomy* names the growing phenomenon of user-generated tagging of digital information with the user's own searchable keywords. These user-generated tags called *folksonomies* are in contrast to taxonomies, which are generally based on rigid directories. The publication of tags for their sharing with others is viewed as an important form of socialization of user-generated content on the Web. (Vossen 183-184)

Folksonomy refers to a form of organic categorization that comes from Internet users as they encounter new information. When you are looking at an image or a Web site, you may think of a number of key descriptive words that help you remember that resource. These keyword descriptions are referred to as tagging a resource. (D'Souza 8)

Folksonomy (also, known by such terms as collaborative tagging, social classification, social indexing, and social tagging) is the collaborative practice and method creating of managing tags to annotate and categorize content information. Folksonomy tagging is intended to make a body of information increasingly easy to search, discover and navigate. A well-developed folksonomy can be accessible as a shared vocabulary that is both originated by, and familiar to, its primary users.

Combining user-generated tags with software makes the categorization of resources relatively simple so you can create a personal searchable database of information. By doing the extra work it takes to organize your own resources, you are sharing the workload in organizing information on the Internet. When you look at all of these personal databases as a whole, patterns begin to emerge where similar resources have similar tags.

Manually created meta-tags are recently seeing a revival in the form of tagging. Users may attach any number of keywords to an object or a Web resource such as an entire Web site, a photo, video or a link. A major difference to the use of meta-tags within Web pages is that tags, although created by individuals, are frequently used within online communities. Tags can be made available and visible to other users, so that when searching through the tags they may adopt them for their own use.

As folksonomies develop on Internet-mediated social environments, users can generally discover who created a given folksonomy, and see the other tags this person created. In this way, folksonomy users discover the tag sets of another user who tends to interpret and tag content in a way that makes sense to them. The result is often an immediate and rewarding gain in the user's capacity to find related content.

ADVANTAGES OF TAGGING AND FOLKSONOMY

Tagging allows users to include associated concepts without wondering whether he has categorized the item in the correct folder or not. Applying structured taxonomies is frustrating because some items do not fit comfortably into any category. This lack of fit especially happens if the concept or product is so new that no terms describing the topic have been added to the taxonomy yet. In comparison, folksonomies are nimble and flexible. They can change quickly. You can add new terms at will, and there is no need to jump through several hoops to get new terms added or approved. (Fichter 43-44)

By using folksonomies, one discovers new and more current digital content due to its ability to be updated immediately. Folksonomies can also be organized so one can explore the "long tail interests" – the less frequently used keywords people choose can help users focus their searches and applications. Tag clouds and folksonomies automatically help create communities as users with similar interests gravitate toward similar, searchable word tags. Tagged content increases the amount of usable retrievals by providing more than one place you can look for information on the same topic.

Best of all, tag clouds and folksonomy are mobile and can be accessed from anywhere with an Internet connection. Educators, students, parents, and other Internet searchers can continue their research regardless of their location.

Folksonomies lend themselves to exploration as well as being self-moderating and inclusive. They are less expensive to maintain than a traditional taxonomy and everyone can contribute to its development.

CHALLENGES WITH TAGGING AND FOLKSONOMY

While the advantages of using tagging, tag clouds and folksonomy far out-weigh the disadvantages, it is important to be aware of some common problems typical of using these Web 2.0 tools. One of the most common problems is the misspelling of tags within the tag cosmos. The result is that it leaves orphaned content that has little benefit to the group at large.

Everyone has different perceptions of what she is reading. Individual tags may tend to be disjointed, irrelevant and often very messy. They lack precision and there is no ability to control synonyms or related terms. Tag clouds and folksonomies contain many variants such as plural, singular, spelling errors, and typos. Different social software tools take different approaches to tags composed of multiple words resulting in even more variations. Folksonomies lack hierarchy. The flat-system folksonomies lack parent-child relationships, categories and subcategories. This lack of hierarchy can directly influence searching and search results. Without hierarchy or synonym control, a search of a specific term will only yield results on that term and not provide the full body of related terms that might be relevant to the user's information needs and goals. Folksonomy does not include "See" and "See Also" guidelines that librarians are familiar with in traditional taxonomy subject classification. Students will need to be mindful of synonyms in a folksonomy that might relate to their topic without having clues provided for them.

Tags with more than one meaning can lead the searcher into an unrelated area. Personalized tags are clear to a handful of people, but are not universally understood. Some may argue that metadata systems already exist and a less structured system is not necessary.

TAG SELECTION PROCESS

The selection of appropriate tags is crucial to the sharing and retrieving of relevant tags and tag clouds. In preparing tags, the most important factor is to identify the central concept of the source. Computers are programmed to match strings of characters and spaces and do not often understand the natural language we use with each other. They cannot guess what the creator means; they do not "read" subtexts, and are easily confused by ambiguity. It is important to clarify for them what the user will be looking for. Focus only on essential concepts.

DIFFERENCES BETWEEN TAGS AND CATEGORIES

In selecting tags for a Web 2.0 application there is a difference between a tag and a category. Categories organize, hierarchically. Tags do not. Tags provide meta-information; Categories do not. Categories can be tags, but not all categories are tags, and not all tags should be categories. Categories are best imagined as a paper filing system. Each page in the system must be filed in the appropriate drawer. There are only a set number of drawers, and so each must cover a rather wide blanket.

Categories can also be compared to a table of contents while tags can be compared to the index page of a book. If a user is searching for a broad topic, unsure of exactly what he needs to find or a specific keyword to use, then he can select the table of contents (categories). If he knows the exact word he needs to find the information he wants, then he can select the index page (tags).

Depending on Web site, tags can link to related tag categories or other tag sites, showing a collection of *offsite posts* from around the web all related to the tag category. Tags can link to a generated page such as your searches do, listing all of the posts *on your site* related to that specific tag. Tags can be linked from within the text, via a list at the bottom of the post, in a list in your sidebar or elsewhere on your site, or within a Tag Cloud.

The drawbacks to tag-based systems is that there are no standard set of keywords (also known as controlled vocabulary) and no standard for the structure of such tags (e.g. singular vs. plural, capitalization, etc.). Wrong tags often occur due to spelling errors, tags can have more than one meaning, and tags can be unclear due to synonym/antonym confusion. Some taggers can develop highly unorthodox and "personalized" tag schemas from the mainstream, and no mechanism for users to indicate hierarchical relationships between tags exists.

GENERATING TAG CLOUDS

Almost any text can be used to create a cloud in a tag cloud generator. You can try the Tag Cloud tool by typing or pasting text into the input box or providing a URL for a public Web site. Tag Cloud tools generate the cloud by removing punctuation, calculating term frequencies, selecting the font sizes to display, and displaying it in a graphic style format.

Several web applications are available to help generate a tag cloud. Popular tag cloud generators include such sites as:

- TagCloud (http://tagcloud.com/)
- TextTagCloud (http://www.artviper.net/texttagcloud/)
- TagCrowd (http://tagcrowd.com/)
- The Tag Cloud Builder from OCLC (Online Catalog Library Center) (http://tagcloud.oclc.org/).

IMPROVING TAG LITERACY

Two key ways in which the metadata created in folksonomies can be improved to aid searching are by educating users to add *better* tags and improving the systems that allow *better* tags to be added. Currently most users do not give much thought to the way they tag resources, and bad or "sloppy" tags abound in folksonomies.

When consider tagging resources, the user needs first to consider the ways that resource will be useful to those who use the system. Most likely, people will not spend a lot of time trying to guess all the possible tags that someone might look for, but there is usually a common vocabulary used within a particular community. Students need to recognize that tags can be both personal and social. In other words, tags can be strictly for one's own use or they can be used by others in the network. Sometimes the same tag can serve both purposes. There are times the user will need to use one kind of tags for his individual purposes, and another kind of tags for a social purpose.

Another guideline to consider in selecting tags is to use plurals to define categories. When appropriate, instead of *wiki* or *cat*, use *wikis* and *cats*. Tags signify a category that can encompass various resources, so the plural form is generally more appropriate. This will avoid having to check both the singular and plural version of a tag. However, sometimes having both a singular and a plural tag is necessary. Until taggers become more consistent in their word selection, tag searchers are often wise to check both the singular and plural forms of their search for possible resources since tagging novices can often contribute vital information on a given topic.

Generally, users should also avoid capitalization in a tag, except when capitalization is the norm. Some tag cloud applications may be case sensitive and others are not.

When selecting tags, students need to think both specific and general. They need to select tags that describe their resource in very specific terms for a specialized group of people, but also consider using tags that describe their resource in general terms for the novice on that topic. Some terms might be too broad to benefit some, but they might be the exact word to help others find their resource. For example, a user who happens to be an auto mechanic who is tagging a blog about a car might use specific tags for the specific parts of a car, but other times using general tags such as *steering* and *braking* would help non-mechanical searchers find the information discussed in the blog.

It is also wise to include as many synonyms as possible that relate to the topic. For example, it may be sufficient for students to tag something with the tag *house*, but other times they may need to spend a couple of extra seconds to include the tags *home, residence,* etc. knowing that those tags have a broad social value. Of course, sometimes synonyms can dilute the associations students wish to make, so if they mean *cinema* and not *film,* then they should use whatever word fits their needs.

Users should observe the norms of the online application or network they are using. How does the application handle compound words? What are the tagging conventions followed by other members of the network? If they make sense to the user, they should adopt them. Many good ideas can come from observing the tagging practices of others.

SUMMARY

Tags, tag clouds, and folksonomies are terms that are often used interchangeably with only minor variations. These tools provide the connectivity and networking of the Web 2.0 applications that will be discussed in later chapters. They are the entryway to the Semantic Web.

The selection of descriptive keywords as tags for folksonomies has broadened the searchability of digital media beyond traditional taxonomies such as Dewey Classification System, Sears Subject Headings, and Library of Congress Subject Headings. Helping users understand the basic principles behind tag clouds and folksonomy, choose relevant tag words, and search for digital materials using folksonomies is critical in helping prepare them for 21st century collaboration, research, and communications skills.

Chapter 4

SOCIAL BOOKMARKING

WHAT IS SOCIAL BOOKMARKING?

Before Web 2.0, when a person discovered a Web site she wanted to refer to later without continually retyping the URL, she simply bookmarked it in her browser. The next time the user needed that particular site she would go to the bookmark folder and click on that link. This worked well if the user only worked on one computer. However, when someone had bookmarked a site on one computer, it was only available on that specific computer. When that person worked on different computer either at home or at work, the saved bookmarks were not available and the user was constantly searching for the same site, rebuilding her favorites list and retyping URLs.

Another problem with storing bookmarks in the browser of a local computer is that users are not able to share their bookmarks with others, and others cannot share their bookmarks with them. The concept of shared online bookmarks dates back to April 1996 with the launch of itList.com. (http://en.wikipedia.org/wiki/Social_bookmarking) Sharing bookmarks is a way for Internet users to organize, store, share and search bookmarks of Web pages on similar topics.

With social, or shared, bookmarking the users save their URLs to a public bookmarking site and *tag* them with keywords. This practice of saving bookmarks to a public Web site and "tagging" them with keywords, results in a user-directed, *amateur* method of classifying information. Because social bookmarking services indicate who created each bookmark and provide access to that person's bookmarked resources. With that information, users can easily make social connections with other individuals interested in similar topics.

Visitors to social bookmarking sites can search for resources by keyword, person or popularity and see the public bookmarks, tags, and classification schemes that registered users have created and saved. Users can also see how many people have used a tag and can search for all resources that have been assigned to that particular tag. In this way, over time the community of users with similar interests will develop a unique structure of keywords to define resources—something that has come to be known as a *folksonomy*.

ADVANTAGES OF SOCIAL BOOKMARKING

The advantages of bookmarking sites that contain user-selected "tagging" terms far outweigh traditional automated resource location and classification software. The traditional automated search engine spiders such as those used by Google and Yahoo, attempt to determine the meaning of a resource by using a complex computer-generated algorithm. When using the tagging format the selection of terms is made by a person who understands the content of the resource.

As large groups of people with similar interests bookmark resources they find useful, the more popular resources will be used and bookmarked more frequently than other URLs.

Such a system will "rank" a resource based on its perceived utility and the value of a site is determined by its popularity and usage.

When users register for a social bookmarking site, they must designate whether the bookmarks are public or private. Most online bookmarks sites are public, but depending on the service's features, bookmarks may be saved privately, shared only with specific people or groups, shared only inside certain networks, or a combination of public and private. The allowed users can view their bookmarks chronologically, by category or tags, via a search engine, or even randomly.

Users can assign as many tags to a Web site URL as they like. As they add more URLs to their social bookmarks, they will undoubtedly use many of the same tag words, as well as create new tags. Social bookmarking site users can quickly find specific Web sites by searching through their tag list and seeing which sites fall under the categories they had assigned. Some social bookmarking sites periodically verify that bookmarks still work and notify users when a URL no longer functions.

SOCIAL BOOKMARK SITES

BACKFLIP

Backflip was one of the first social bookmarking services that allowed users to organize, search, and share links. Netscape veterans Tim Hickman and Chris Misner started it in 1999, but ended in financial trouble during the dot-com bubble burst in 2000. However, it was sold to a group of employees who kept it going and volunteers are now running the service. (Pick)

Figure 4:1 – Backflip Screenshot

To use Backflip, all it takes is a click, and whenever a user finds interesting Web pages, he can depend on easily getting back to those sites, no matter how many he has saved. To share folders with others you simply need to enter the email addresses of those who may be interested and Backflip takes care of the rest. Those interested are notified and they can view the selected Web pages, whether they are Backflip members or not. Users can make comments, view each other's comments, and if they choose, they can contribute more pages that are interesting.

DIGG

Digg is a social Web site like MySpace and Facebook, where users interact with each other. One of the main reasons Digg is so popular is because it can drive thousands of visitors to a Web site within minutes. Its emphasis is on news articles covering technology, science, politics and entertainment.

Digg (http://digg.com) began as an experiment in November 2004 by Kevin Rose, Owen Byrne, Ron Gorodetzky and Jay Adelson. The founders named their new site "Digg" because users are able to "dig" stories out of those submitted. "Dig" as a name could not be used because the domain name "dig.com" was previously registered.

Figure 4:2 - Digg Screenshot

You can do two main things on Digg. The first is to submit stories that you think the community will like and the second is to 'digg' stories other users like. There are currently seven categories on Digg, which include technology, science, world and business, sports, videos, entertainment, and gaming. If you come across any stories you find interesting, you can submit them to Digg for others to vote on. If a user likes a story, they have the option of "digging" it, which consists of voting on it and endorsing it. However, if they do not like a story then they can bury it by marking it as duplicate, spam, wrong topic, inaccurate or even lame. If they would like to say more, a comment section gives the users an opportunity to add their thoughts on the topic.

DELICIOUS

Delicious (http://deliciouscom/), (formerly **del.icio.us**,

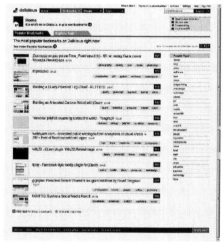

Figure 4:3 – delicious Screenshot

pronounced "delicious") which is owned by Yahoo!, is currently one of the most popular social bookmarking sites. Users can apply 'delicious' by saving links to their favorite articles, blogs, music, reviews, recipes, and more, and then access them from any computer on the web as well as share favorites with friends, family, coworkers, and the entire delicious community.

If you want to keep their individual bookmarks hidden from others, you need to first allow it, and then choose the "do not share" checkbox when editing or saving an item.

Not only can you access their own stored bookmarks, you can browse and search delicious to discover useful bookmarks others have saved or send private communications to other users.

If it is important to remain up to date on what people are currently bookmarking with a specific tag, you can subscribe to RSS feeds containing that category and tag. Instead of searching for your own Web sites on a topic with a traditional search engine, you can now share the work and see the Web sites other people with similar interests have used.

A user's collection is found at the address, (http://delicious.com/username) and has the RSS of (http://delicious/rss/username). We can follow certain user's collections and sub-collections, characterized by tags by subscribing to the RSS of the users' collection. By adding a user to our own network at (http://delicious/network/username) we can find the resources that were added by all users from that username's network. (Grosseck)

To record a URL from the browser into "delicious," you must first register for the service from a toolbar button and download a bookmarklet from https://secure.delicious/register. When the "delicious" bookmarklet on the toolbar is activated the "Bookmark This Page" icon is activated, a pop-up form appears with the URL fields and the site's title/description is automatically filled in.

To make the greatest use of the tags, after a few entries it is helpful to bundle the tags. With tags in the correct bundle, it makes the tagged Web sites much easier to find.

FURL

Furl (from File Uniform Resource Locators) from Looksmart is a free social bookmarking Web site (furl.net) that allows members to store searchable copies of Web pages and share them with others. Every member receives 5 gigabytes of storage space.

The key to using Furl is that you need a button in your browser that you can click to save the item you are viewing. Thanks to technology called *bookmarklets*, you do not need to install any software to do this. Once you have the button in the toolbar of your browser, you can continue to use the Internet as you normally would. Whenever you find something of interest,

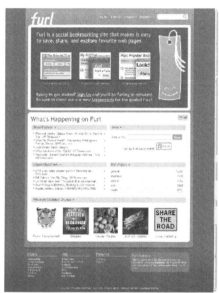

Figure 4:4 – Furl Screenshot

you merely click the "Furl It" button to add the page to your archive. A pop-up box will provide you the option to add comments, categorize and date the item before you click "Save."

The unique feature of Furl is that it privately archives a snapshot of the entire page of the HTML of each page that a user bookmarks as opposed to saving just the URL. This method makes it accessible even if the original content is modified or removed; that means the end of *link rot*. Full text searches can be made within the archive, but images that are embedded links will not be archived with the HTML page. To avoid claims of copyright violations, this archived copy is visible only to the member who bookmarked the page. Other users are directed to the publisher's site, where the content can be viewed depending on membership requirements and privacy settings.

You may see lists of other users who have furled a URL, and read their comments (if made public) to find users who share similar interests. A dynamic recommendation list is available to each user, automatically based on the sites already saved others with similar interests. You can subscribe to a specific FURL and receive email updates when new content is added to that particular FURL or view the Furl feed in a news aggregator using the RSS feed.

The power of FURL is its *searchability*. When you bookmark a site with Furl, others can search using the keywords you created, words you used in your comments and clippings, plus you can search by date and by topic.

DIIGO

Diigo (http://www.diigo.com/) offers a powerful personal tool that goes beyond adding bookmarks and tags. Diigo turns the entire web into a writable, participatory, and interactive media by combining social bookmarking, clippings, annotations, tagging, full-text search, easy sharing and interactions. All user created tags can be subscribed to by those interested in the same topic using an RSS feed that is updated in real-time whenever anyone saves a URL using a particular Diigo tag. From their toolbar, users can simultaneously save links in nine different bookmarking services.

The name "Diigo" is an abbreviation for *Digest of Internet Information, Groups and Other stuff.* Diigo (dee'go) is about *Social Annotation*. This program allows you to highlight all or part of a page and attach sticky notes to that page. Diigo's annotations can be kept private, shared with a group within Diigo, or a specific link can be forwarded to someone else. Diigo displays as a giant transparency overlaying on top of all the Web pages. Users can highlight passages

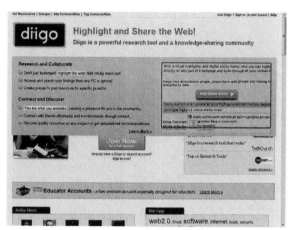

Figure 4:5– Diigo Screenshot

and write on the transparency, as private notes or public comments, and read public comments on the transparency left by other readers of the same page.

In earlier versions, a sticky note had to be tied to a highlighted section. On recent versions, you can also add a "floating" sticky note that does not have to be associated with any highlight. You can move the sticky note around and position it anywhere you wish on a Web page by simply clicking "Sticky Note" icon on the new toolbar (found in Toolbar Options), or in the right-click menu.

With one-click 'Blog This' on the context menu or toolbar they can instantaneously convert their Diigo highlights and sticky notes into a blog account in one of these blog host sites -- WordPress, Blogger, LiveJournal, TypePad, Movable Type, or Windows Live Spaces account. Users no longer need to copy and paste text when they edit and publish a new post based on the content of interesting Web pages they have selected. Another strong feature of Diigo is that its bookmarks and tags synchronize with Delicious.

CITEULIKE

For academic and professional development work, educators may want to consider CiteULike social bookmarking service. CiteULike (http://www.citeulike.org/) is an online tool based in the United Kingdom designed to help scientists, researchers, and academics store, organize, share and discover links to academic research papers. As of late 2007, CiteULike contained 2,002,290 journal articles.

You can browse current issues of many research journals or import articles from repositories while the online service will attempt to determine the article metadata (title, authors, journal name, etc) automatically. You can organize your libraries with freely chosen tags, which produce a domain-specific folksonomy of academic interests. CiteULike also allows you to see what other people posted publicly, which tags they added, and how they commented and rated a paper. CiteULike groups allow individual users to collaborate with other users to build a library of references. RSS feeds and Watch lists allow users to track tags and users' libraries that interest them, showing the latest additions to their chosen categories.

CiteULike fuses two separate categories of software: the new 'Web 2.0' breed of social bookmarking services and traditional bibliographic management software (EndNote - http://www.endnote.com/). While Web bookmarks are simple URLs, citations are a bit more complex and include metadata like journal names, authors, page numbers etc. *EndNote Web* is a Web-based service designed to help students and researchers through the process of writing a research paper.

Desktop software such as EndNote allows you to collect the articles that you wish to keep for future reference. The collection process stores sufficient metadata for the article (the title, authors, journal name, and page number) in a bibliographic format that allows for its ultimate sharing with others by citing it in the author's own publication.

EDUCATIONAL USES OF SOCIAL BOOKMARKS

Educators are discovering innumerable ways to use social bookmarking to help students meet their educational standards and goals. Small groups and entire classes can use bookmarking services such as FURL for collaboration. A group account can be established, with the password shared with the participants or, in what is probably a safer and more useful version; a group can establish a unique tag and tag all group-related links with it.

For individual projects, teachers can save the URLs of pages for students to read. To access their reading assignments, students can use a news aggregator to view their new postings automatically from school, home, or wherever they may have an Internet connection.

Using social bookmarking sites, students can take control of selecting and archiving their own resources on a given topic and sharing those links with their classmates.

Many bookmarking sites allow teachers to review and comment on resources the students have bookmarked. This collaboration feature is the strength of social bookmarking as it permits both teachers and students to collaborate with web resources. Everyone can contribute to a project as well as reap the benefits of teamwork.

Using a bookmarking site, such as Diigo that allows users to post notes directly on the Web page, teachers can set up a group account per each class. They are then able to verify if a student has read an online article or if they have understood what they read by the notes they posted on the Web page. A screencast tutorial in setting up a Diigo account is located at http://www.screencast-o-matic.com/watch/cij0ev4l.

Some schools have expanded the usefulness of the school Web page by placing web links of a bookmarking site directly onto their school Web page. The visitors to their site are then alerted to any updates of news that is relevant to the school's mission and environment.

The school Web site can be used to track author and book updates and can immediately notify web viewers when a new book by a particular author is released. Some schools like to share bookmarking accounts between different subject specific educators in a school in order to share resources with each other. Others like to share one account between a large number of educators across a school district that teach in diverse settings in order to create a broad and deep set of resources.

Some bookmarking sites such as FURL provide citation services that will create a bibliography on a new Web page so you can cut and paste the bibliography into your document. Users can select from MLA, APA or Chicago Style bibliography format.

SOCIAL CATALOGING

LIBRARYTHING.COM

LibraryThing is a social network of bibliophiles. It is a Web site to help people catalog their own books, as well as connect people with the same books in their libraries, and provides suggestions for what to read next. LibraryThing's primary feature is the automatic cataloging of books by importing data from booksellers and libraries through Z39.50 (Z39.50 is a client server protocol for searching and retrieving information from remote computer databases). August 2005, Tim Spalding developed LibraryThing. As of January 2009, Library Thing had 581,980 registered users who had cataloged 34,264,409 books with 44,403,767 tags.

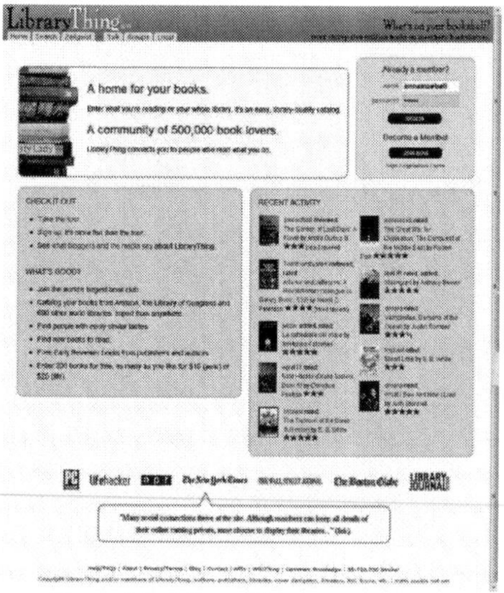

Figure 4:6 - LibraryThing

The LibraryThing Web site does not use advertising, but receives referral fees from online bookstores that supply book cover images. Individual users can sign up for free and register up to 200 books. Beyond that limit and/or for commercial or group use, a subscription fee is charged. You can browse LibraryThing at no cost and can post up to 200 books at no charge. You can also access your virtual library from your cell phone while standing in a bookstore by pointing your cell phone's browser to (http://www.librarything.com/m). Beyond that, users have to pay either $10 for a yearly membership or $25 for a lifetime account.

LibraryThing users (informally known as thingamabrarians) can catalog personal collections, keep reading lists, and meet other users who have the same books. While it is possible to keep a library catalog private, most people choose to make their catalogs public, which makes it possible to find others with similar tastes. Thingamabrarians can browse the entire database by searching titles, authors, or tags generated by other users as they enter books into their own libraries.

Users of LibraryThing can import information from over 80 libraries including the Library of Congress, and the Canadian National Catalogue. Once the correct book and edition has been located, a simple click adds it to their own catalog. They can also add books from another member's catalog or by searching on LibraryThing itself. Assuming the book is found (and most will be), each time a user adds a book, LibraryThing automatically posts an image of its front cover, its date of publication, its ISBN (International Standard Book Number), and a list of other editions. It may even suggest where a person can buy new copies online. If users desires, they can add other information, including tags, a star rating, a Dewey decimal number, the date they acquired the book, the day they started reading, and the date they finished reading it. Users can add comments to the database and even post reviews. If the correct book or edition is not available, users can add it manually or edit the record later.

Although LibraryThing provides cataloging data from the Library of Congress, it encourages its users to tag the books included in their collective collections. LibraryThing, like many other folksonomy applications, incorporates a tag cloud into the "Social Information" page created for each book.

When a book is tagged, users can view when others use the same tag. The section *Members with Your Books* shows the 50 most similar libraries from other members. When viewing another member's profile or library, the system shows how many (and which) books you share with that other member. If desired, you can leave a (public or private) comment on their profile. You can also add the member as a friend, to your private watch list, or as an interesting library.

Both LibraryThing and Amazon allow users to tag books. However, with only a fraction of Amazon's traffic, LibraryThing has accumulated ten times as many book tags as Amazon. This could be explained by the fact that tagging works well when people tag their own possessions, but it fails when they are asked to do it to someone else's. Traditional library OPACs (Online Public Access Catalog) lack mechanisms to collect the knowledge of library patrons. The classification schemes used to organize library collections rely on the expertise of few specialists with detailed knowledge of the Dewey Decimal system, the Library of Congress classification system, and the Library of Congress or Sears subject headings. Although these formal systems work well as far as it goes, a Library 2.0 catalog that could generate additional metadata from the combined wisdom of library patrons would enhance the value of the OPAC. A library catalog that could point users to "recommended" titles in the collection based on the reading habits and the descriptions of their fellow patrons would be a great benefit to many readers. (Wenzler)

Danbury Public Library, Danbury, Connecticut was the first library to add the LibraryThing widgets to its catalog. The LibraryThing data is integrated almost seamlessly into the record display. Tags and the tag browsers bring the cataloging efforts of LibraryThing's thousands of users into the local OPAC. Users merely click on a tag associated with a book and the tag browser opens and provides a list of all the other books in the library with that same tag. The tag browser also provides a tag search engine, which has created an entirely new way to navigate the catalog. (http://cat.danburylibrary.org/)

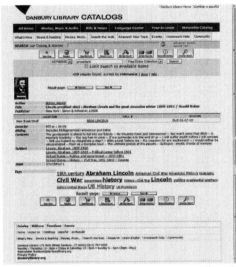

Figure 4:7 – Danbury OPAC

Depending on their OPAC vendor, libraries have a great deal of freedom in controlling how and where the LibraryThing widgets display in the record. The links use the ISBN search interface of the catalog to take patrons to similar books.

LibraryThing does most of the work required to set up a LibraryThing widget on an OPAC, but there is some work for the OPAC administrator. There are four basic steps in the process from the perspective of the library.

1. Sign up for a library account:
   (http://www.librarything.com/forlibraries)
2. Upload a file of the ISBNs in the library catalog to
   LibraryThing.
3. Configure the widgets on the LibraryThing site.
   Libraries have control over how many tags and
   recommendations will appear in the record.
4. Add the widgets to the record display in the library
   catalog. The widgets are added by inserting a link to a
   JavaScript file that LibraryThing writes specifically for
   each library that signs up for the service.

SHELFARI

Another interesting social cataloging site is Shelfari
(http://www.shelfari.com), which was launched October
2006 by Kevin Bukelman and Josh Hug. Shelfari
introduces readers to a global community of book lovers
and encourages them to share their literary passions with
peers, friends, and total strangers.

The community of Shelfari users, known as Shelfarians,
enjoys the basic features such as Personalized Book
Shelves, Social Interaction, Book Discovery, and Intuitive
Tagging. A comment section is designed to facilitate asking
others within Shelfari a question about any book. Shelfari
makes its money when users find new books and order
through Shelfari on Amazon or another service. Shelfari
also has some limited advertising.

Shelfarians are able to further expand their reading
communities by adding a Shelfari widget on their personal
blog, Facebook, or My Space account and display the
books in their Shelfari shelf. Users can edit the widget size,
book size, background color, and even add their Amazon
Associates ID so they can make money from books bought

through the traffic they send to Shelfari. Shelfari (unlike LibraryThing) allow for an unlimited number of books on a users Internet shelf free of charge.

Figure 4:8 Shelfari

After adding a book to their personal bookshelf, Shelfarians are able to assign tags to that book. A personal Tag Cloud appears below the user's bookshelf and profile page as soon as they have created their first tag. Newly added tags connect with the same tags already in the database and group these books together. Selecting a tag within a Tag Cloud will display the collection of books associated with that tag so users can determine when they have something in common with other readers using Shelfari.

LISTAL

Listal (http://www.listal.com/) is a London-based social network centered on entertainment and media collections created by Tom Mascord. On this site you can list movies, music, games, TV, DVDs, and books as well as tag, rate and review, recommend and share lists with friends. You can also track loans, view statistics for their collection, plus search, sort and filter their collection. RSS feeds are available for all lists.

Recently Listal has launched actor profiles so you can view actor photos and videos (from YouTube), rate them, tag them, add comments, and become a fan. Similar features have been added for bands and artists. Products can be added to Listal via search of Amazon Standard Identification Number (ASIN) or ISBN (for books).

SUMMARY

The use of tags, tag clouds, and folksonomy has provided an exciting resource and tool for storing and sharing information via the Internet. Students, educators, and librarians who have adopted social bookmarking and social cataloging have been able to reduce the time doing online research as they have improved the relevancy of the resources they found. Users appreciate the ability to share their research as opposed to doing all the research themselves.

Social cataloging provides a way for book lovers not only to catalog their personal libraries, but also to network with those with the same literary interests. Students can be encouraged to set up their own personal bookshelves and write reviews on the books they have read. Some libraries are beginning to take advantage of the informal tag selection of individuals as well as the traditional taxonomy of the Library of Congress or Sears Subject Headings to assist users retrieve relevant resources.

Chapter 5

PHOTO SHARING

WHAT IS PHOTO SHARING?

Millions of digital cameras in the hands of the curious and creative have led to billions of images waiting to be shared. Online photo sharing services make organizing, storing, and sharing digital photos convenient, easy, and safe. Through photo albums, friends and family can share pictures of important events, good times, and special occasions, while students and photographers that are more serious can display their work and make it available for others to use. The same technology that allows digital photographs to be shared can be used for other electronic image formats such as computer-generated art or scans of hand-drawn artwork or photographic prints.

Photo-sharing sites can be broadly broken up into two groups: sites that offer free photo sharing and sites that charge consumers directly to host and share photos. Paid sites typically offer subscription-based services directly to consumers and withhold advertisements and the sale of other goods. These designations are not hard and fast and some subscription sites have a limited free version and charge for more storage space. The benefits to the consumer of paid photo sharing are that the company may offer greater guarantees about keeping the photos online and allow friends and family to download the full-size original files. They are also a great way to backup pictures.

ONLINE PHOTO FINISHING

Because printing at home for consumers is potentially time consuming, costly, or low quality, a number of providers offer the ability to create high quality prints from digital photos, printed digitally on photographic paper. Typically, the customer uploads their digital photos to the site and orders prints and gifts, which are then delivered by mail. Users can create shirts, luggage tags, mugs, cards, calendars, clothing, tiles, books, or even edible chocolate photos and have the service send the gift anywhere they choose. To facilitate the sale of prints and gifts to family and friends, these sites typically offer a limited form of photo sharing.

Common online photo finishing sites include Kodak Gallery (http://www.kodakgallery.com), Fastlab.com (http://www.fastlab.com), Photoworks.com (http://www.photoworks.com), and Snapfish.com (http://www.snapfish.com).

PHOTO SHARING SITES

Each photo sharing service is different, but they all offer upload forms with the ability to browse to images on one's own computer, so users can select the images they would like to share. They all post images to a Web site on the Internet; except for Picasa, which shares images over the Internet and uses their own computer to host them.

Most photo sharing sites contain the ability to classify photos into albums as well as add annotations, captions, and comments. Some photo-sharing sites provide complete online organization tools equivalent to desktop photo-management applications. Many photo-sharing services also offer services and space where tight–knit groups or communities can come together and share photographs and exchange ideas about photography. Users can post their pictures for public or private view where other members can offer feedback on their pictures. These sites publish engaging, professional and beautiful images of people and places from around the world for browsing and comment.

Viewbook (http://www.viewbook.com) is a web-based service that you can use to create albums, presentations, and portfolios. Uploading images is fast and easy by merely dragging and dropping pictures (jpg, png, ANF, gif formats) and arranging them to create image slideshows that you can share via email or embed on their Web site or blog.

Google's Picasa (http://picasa.google.com) is a popular photo-sharing and powerful basic editing software. The new WebAlbum photo-sharing element makes Picasa a one-stop solution for photo editing and sharing. With WebAlbum and the Picasa software, users can upload entire albums of high quality photos with a click of the software's "Web Album" button, or with their normal web browser to add pictures.

Shutterfly (http://www.shutterfly.com) not only delivers quality prints from a user's digital camera right to their door, it offers a multitude of gift and book printing options. This site provides free online photo storage and sharing. Their free photo software, Shutterfly Studio lets you easily organize, edit, and share your picture collections directly from your desktop. You can enhance your prints for free with colorful, festive and seasonal borders and add personalized captions. Every photo ordered from Shutterfly can be personalized for free with a short message on the reverse side.

One of the largest and best-known photo-sharing Web sites is Flickr (http://www.flickr.com). Flickr uses an advertising supported model so users can publish their images free of charge. For those interested in more features, Flickr Pro costs $24.95 and provides unlimited storage, uploads, bandwidth, and sets along with permanent archiving of high-resolution original sets. Flickr (owned by Yahoo) has a huge community of users along with a great many free browser plug-ins and software packages to enhance Flickr shared photos.

TAGGING PHOTOS

Most photo-sharing sites provide a taxonomy where images can be grouped within a directory-like structure in so-called *galleries*. However, most sites also allow users to classify images using tags to build a folksonomy. Tags are like keywords or labels that you add to a photo to make it easier to locate later. In searching the database of tags, you can simply click that tag and retrieve all the photos that have been tagged with the same word. Many services allow you to add tags to the photos that others have submitted providing it is permitted through the privacy settings.

There are about 20 million unique tags on Flickr today. To use tags with Flickr, its title, the upload date, and the uploader's name accompany the photo. More recent images from the uploader (called the *photostream),* groups the image to what has been added with the same tags. Additional information (such as license or date on which the photo was shot), and the photo description and comments can also be added.

FLICKR NOTES (HOT-SPOT ANNOTATIONS)

Figure 5:1 – Flickr Notes

One of the most useful tools in Flickr is the annotation feature, which allows you to add notes to parts of the image simply by dragging a box across an area and typing text into a form. Once an image has been published on Flickr, you can press the small add note icon above the image and then draw hotspots on the image and then attach a note to those hotspots. Whenever a user moves their cursor over any of the hotspots, the annotations appear.

ORGANIZING PHOTOS ONLINE

In Flickr, sets are a grouping of photos that you can organize around a certain theme, such as *Our Field Trip* or *Christmas 2008*. You can use sets to highlight your favorite photos, or make an album of a particular activity or location. Collections are a grouping of Sets (or other Collections) so you can organize around larger themes, such as Classes, Activities, or by year (2009, *2008*, *2007*, etc).

Organizr (http://www.flickr.com/photos/organize) is a powerful tool for managing your photos in batches or using sets or you can edit photo-related information one photo at a time. Both collections and sets are created in the Organizr, where you can perform common tasks on large batches of photos, such as tagging, changing permissions, or editing timestamps.

To access Organizr merely click the "Organize" tab at the top of any Flickr page. In Your Photos, click the "Edit this as a batch" link to open Organizr with the batch loaded, you are ready to go. The Organizr Toolbar changes depending on the tab you are working in. Each menu drops down to reveal other options for working with your photos.

The strip on the bottom of the Organizr is the Findr. When you open Organizr the most recent photos will be visible, the newest on the left, the older on the right. To navigate photos in Findr either click the previous and next arrows or drag the slider.

GEOTAGGING PHOTOS

GeoTagging is the process of adding geographical identification metadata to various media such as Web sites, RSS feeds, or images. This data usually consists of latitude and longitude coordinates and place names.

Figure 5.2 Geotagging

You can geotag your photos using Organizr by dragging and dropping them on to the map where you took them. The best way to look at your photos is to go straight to your personal map. Click the "Map" link under your name on your main photos page and place a location for each of your photos.

SHARING PHOTOS

PHOTOCASTING SLIDESHOW TOOLS

Photocasting is a new way of sharing photos accompanied by music and/or narrations. It is sending a photo album to classmates and family, and having the pictures change automatically on their computers.

SlideFlickr (http://slideflickr.com) will help you create and embed Flickr slideshows so you can put slideshows in your own blogs, Web sites, MySpace, or Facebook sites. These slideshows can be generated from sets, groups, or tags of users.

Bubbleshare (http://www.bubbleshare.com) creates slideshows from uploaded images or clip art library and then permits recording thirty seconds of audio/video captions for each image. It also allows overlay comic bubbles with text features. Coding is provided to embed the slideshow in blogs and Web sites.

One True Media (http://www.onetruemedia.com), Slide (http://www.slide.com), Slideroll (http://www.slideroll.com), and RockYou (http://www.rockyou.com) also allow you to combine photos and video clips with words and music to form a multimedia montage. These online sites then create code to be embedded in blogs or posted to YouTube/Google video, MySpace, or Google Groups.

PHOTOBLOGGING

A photoblog (a.k.a. photolog or phlog) is a form of photo sharing and publishing in the format of a blog. The difference is that a photoblog focuses on photographs rather than text. Photoblogging became popular with the advent of the moblog and camera phones.

Many photoblogs only display a chronological view of user-selected medium-sized photos, while other photo sharing sites provide multiple views, such as slideshows and thumbnails. Online photo galleries can be established as photoblogs in which you can organize your photos into sets and several sets can be combined into categories.

Flickr photos can be added to separate blog services such as Yahoo! 360° (http://360.yahoo.com). If you are a Yahoo! 360° user, go to your My Page and click "Share Photos." There you will find a link to share images from your Flickr photostream.

Flickr photos can also be added to a Web site by creating a dynamic badge of public Flickr photos (http://www.flickr.com/badge.gne). You can filter images by a certain tag and choose the display options (which photos, how many, what size) and specify if you want to display your screen name and buddy icon. You have the flexibility to choose either a styled version of the badge (photos appear in a column with a colored background) or one that you can design yourself.

To include Flickr photos on an external blog you need to first configure that blog from (http://www.flickr.com/blogs.gne). The software will guide you through the set-up process. When that is done, you can blog any public photo on Flickr. When you are looking at a single photo such as (http://www.flickr.com/photos/annamaebell/2017202247), you will see a "Blog This" button above it. Click the "Blog This" button for the photo you want to post. If your blog is already set up, you can post immediately by adding a title and body for the post.

Currently Flickr supports the following blogs: Atom Enabled Blogs, Blogger, Blogger API Enabled Blogs, Blogger Beta, LiveJournal, Manila, Meta Weblog API Enabled Blogs, Movable Type, Typepad, Vox, and WordPress.

MOBILE PHOTOBLOGGING

Photo sharing is not confined to the web and personal computers but is also possible from portable devices such as camera phones, using applications that can automatically transfer photos to photo-sharing sites as you take them. You can create photoblogs, either directly or via Multimedia Messaging Service.

To take advantage of this feature you can create your own Flickr mobile account (http://m.flickr.com). The best way to send photos to Flickr from your device is by email and each member of Flickr can get a specific 'Upload2Blog' email address. When you upload a photo to Flickr via email, and you have at least one blog set up in Flickr, your photo can be posted to your blog automatically. When you upload photos via email, you need to use the subject line to give your photo a title, and the body of the email to give it a description.

LEGAL AND SAFETY ISSUES

Most photo sharing sites allow you to use groups and privacy controls to share your photos. The age of the students and the audience anticipated will influence the level of privacy you select.

Flickr accounts are intended for personal use, for our members to share photos that they have taken themselves. Flickr has introduced content filters to help regulate who can view what photos. The safety levels provided are:

1. Safe - *Content suitable for a public audience*
2. Moderate - *It doesn't need to be restricted for some users*
3. Restricted – *Not suitable for children*

To change the filter, you can flag your photo by simply clicking on it. This opens small widgets where you can change the content and safety filters you are applying to each of the images.

Flickr was designed for personal use, not commercial purposes. If they find users selling products or services through a photostream, they will terminate that account. Flickr must approve any commercial use of Flickr technologies or Flickr accounts. Users must not upload anything that is not theirs, including other people's photographs and/or images that have been collected from around the Internet. Flickr does not permit the uploading of content that is illegal or prohibited.

In most parts of the world, including the U.S., Canada, the European countries, and Japan, you are automatically granted copyrights to your own photos upon production. Just because an image is on Flickr or anywhere else on the Internet, does not mean that it is in the public domain.

CREATIVE COMMONS

To help creators protect their intellectual property rights, the nonprofit Creative Commons (http://creativecommons.org) offers an alternative to full copyright. There are over two million photos posted at Flickr that carry Creative Commons copyright licenses, which allow for their legal reuse in any number of ways. You can browse or search through photos under each type of license. Creative Commons currently offers six default licenses as an alternative to full copyright so you can choose the one that best suits your needs.

The levels of copyright licenses Creative Commons offers are:

1. Attribution (others can copy, distribute, display, and perform your copyrighted work - and derivative works based upon it - but only if they give you credit for the work)
2. Attribution-No Derivations License (Let others copy, distribute, display, and perform only verbatim copies of your work, not derivative works based upon it)
3. Attribution-Noncommercial-No Derivations License (Noncommercial will let others copy, distribute, display, and perform your work - and derivative works based upon it - but only for noncommercial purposes)
4. Attribution-Noncommercial License

5. Attribution-Noncommercial-Share Alike License (Share Alike allows others to distribute derivative works only under a license identical to the license that governs your work)
6. Attribution-Share Alike License (http://flickr.com/creativecommons/)

To add a license for a specific picture on Flickr, you need to click the "Change" link next to your current photo license (usually set to "All rights reserved") near the bottom of your photo page. On the Privacy and Permissions settings page, click the "Add a license to your photo" link on the right side of the page, near the bottom. On the next page, select one of the Creative Commons licenses. (http://www.flickr.com/help/photos/?search=creative+com mons#87)

If you applied a Creative Commons license to your photos, they can be downloaded by anyone. If you do not want others to download your photos, remove the Creative Commons license to your images. If you or your students want to use a photo found on Flickr or other photo-sharing site and a Creative Commons License is not available, you need to contact the photographer yourself.

As a member of Flickr, you can move your mouse over someone's buddy icon and click the arrow to open the "person menu." From there select "Send FlickrMail" and compose your message. When you contact a photographer, it is best to include as much information as possible about the photo, yourself, and how you plan to use the photo. Records of the copyright owner's permission should be archived for as long as the photos are in use.

FLICKR IN THE CURRICULUM

In nearly every curriculum area, after students learn how to use tags and tag clouds, they will be able to search for photos of areas and events around the world for use in their classroom and school. Photo-sharing sites can be used to store, promote, and document school events in order to share photos with the school community. Students and educators can also use these sites to create digital portfolios where they can comment on the photos that are included.

Many services such as Flickr allows you to embed photos in a blog, Web site and share them via RSS, which is an excellent way for parents to stay connected with their child's day. Pictures taken on a field trip or school assembly can be uploaded immediately to share with parents who were unable to attend.

Educators can use third party tools such as Flickr Toys (http://bighugelabs.com/flickr) to create motivational and personalized posters, magazine covers, CD covers, and more, by using shared photos. With the advent of the photo-sharing sites, media literacy teachers and students have an abundance of resources to critique and model. They can grab feeds from interesting local photographers and bring them into the classroom for discussion, or for writing inspiration.

Media literacy students can also try a two-part Flickr activity known as "Tell a Story in Five or Six Frames" (http://flickr.com/groups/visualstory). The first part is creating and telling a story through visual means with only five still photos containing only a title to help guide the interpretation. The second part is the response of the group to the visual story.

Another possible application for using photo sharing include having a student in a history class takes a walking tour of a historic building or district and take photographs of various historical or architectural elements. The student can then organize the photos into a set and present a slideshow during an oral report to the class. With the student's permission, the teacher can archive that slideshow to be used with later classes.

A group of science students on a field trip could take photographs of different types of plant life, and then include these as photo illustrations in their written report and share them on the school Web site and tagged carefully in Flickr for future reference. As students work on their projects, they are simultaneously developing writing, technology, photography, and most importantly, collaborative learning skills.

A classroom teacher could travel to a literary or historical site during the summer and then upload his pictures to a photo-sharing site using detailed tagging to meet the objectives of his upcoming classes. Those photos will be able to be referred to whenever necessary throughout the year.

A foreign language teacher could post pictures from her travels to the countries where the language is spoken to provide descriptions of the local color, landscape, and architecture of the area. Students can then practice their language skills by leaving comments and notes on the photographs in that language, thereby putting their use of language in a situated context. Students could also search the global archives for photos tagged with related tags and then discuss how those photographs portray that country's culture.

Students can take pictures of several insects within the same image and then prepare hot spot notes identifying each insect. Their classmates can then run their mouse over the image to activate the pop up containing the name of the individual insects.

SUMMARY

Visual and media literacy is critical for both adults and young people to have a well-balanced understanding of the 21st century environment. The use of photo-sharing sites holds great potential as part of a multi-faceted approach that blends learning theory and social technologies into the curriculum, the business world, and personal networking.

Chapter 6

BLOGGING

WHAT IS A BLOG?

A blog is a Web site in which items are posted on a regular basis and displayed in reverse chronological order. A blog consists of text, hypertext, images, and links to other Web pages and to video, audio, and other files. Blogging is an easy way of publishing your thoughts and ideas to the web.

A blog is similar to an empty book; it is how you use that book, which makes the difference. Your book can be anything you want it to be from a diary, a sketchbook, a dictionary, a novel, or a writing portfolio. It all depends on the content that we put into this book.

> **Blog -** shortened version for the words 'web' and 'log'.

What distinguishes a blog from a read-only Web site is the process. Blogs are not built on static chunks of content like a read-only site, but they contain ideas, reflections, and conversations that are updated regularly. Blogs engage readers with ideas, questions, and links. They ask readers to think and to respond using the commenting feature. (Richards 18) Blogs contain the ability to archive content that is posted by date in reverse chronological order.

Blog software also facilitates syndication through RSS feeds. As soon as a new posting is available, notifications are sent immediately to the subscribers' RSS feed aggregator. This saves time for the readers who will not need to check the Web site regularly to see if the blogger has added another posting.

There are multiple types or blog genres. Here are the most common:

1. Personal diary - You can blog about what you do every day or about things you think about or dreams you have for the future.
2. News blogs - Contain what bloggers think about what is going on in the world or in a given interest area.
3. Activist blogs – Advocate of a specific attempts to rally the masses for a particular cause.
4. Political blogs – Promote the views of a specific politician or political ideal. Many politicians' careers have risen or fallen on the strength of their blog or the blogs of others.
5. Education blogs – Contain resources for ideas and best practices within the educational environment.
6. Technology blogs – Discuss the latest news and ideas in the field of technology.
7. Corporate and industry blogs - Provide opportunities to get their message out and communicate with customers.
8. Celebrities and gossip blogs
9. Hobby blogs

ANATOMY OF A BLOG

There can be wide differences between the layouts of individual blogs, but there are definite features most blogs share. The common characteristics that blogs share regardless of the genre include:

- A subject or header similar to a newspaper article, or e-mail
- A body or content section
- A comment section where the readers have a chance to respond to what is written
- A time and date stamp - so that readers know how recent the post is

Another important feature that is common to most blogs is the trackbacks. When you publish a posting to your blog, it gets its very own URL to distinguish it from the other postings. When someone types this URL into their browser or clicks a link from your blog index page, they are transported to that particular posting. Most blog publishing platforms will scan every link in every posting you publish.

If you have linked to a blog that is accepting trackbacks, then it will send a small data packet known as a ping over the Internet to that blog. This has the effect of notifying the blog in question that someone is talking about them, prompting its software to add a comment of its own to the original post saying, in effect, someone else is talking about me and here's a direct link to them.

The important issue is that you do not have to know how trackbacks work in order to be able to benefit from the technology. Just check your blogging software options, or refer to the support documentation, and make sure you enable posts to receive trackbacks and the job is done for you. Most blogging software will even e-mail you a notification whenever a new trackback has been observed, treating it in exactly the same way as it does a local comment.

There are several advantages to commenting on other blogs. When you post comments on someone else's blog, your comments should be relevant to the topic discussed. They can be informative, funny or just a nod of agreement. It is your way of giving back to the blogging community as a whole. Your comment should not be about your own blog, although most bloggers will not object if you leave a link to your blog in your signature line. Many blog hosts even provide a place for you to leave your blog's URL within the comments.

Linking and commenting back and forth is an excellent way to get your blog noticed by other bloggers, and will raise your ranking in a search engine. This linking between blogs is a key reason why blogs are different from personal Web sites. You can turn off the comments section on most blog hosting sites. However, unless you do not want to interact with the world and the blogging community for a specific reason, it is recommended you leave comments turned on. Comments let you know what your readers are thinking and what they would like to see on your blog. If you give them more of what they want, they are more likely to come back to your blog again.

A permalink is a permanent URL that is generated by the blogging system and is applied to each individual post. Even if the item is moved within the database for archiving, the permalink remains the same. Because a permalink remains unchanged indefinitely, it is less susceptible to link rot.

A blogroll is a list of links to other blogs that a particular blogger likes or finds useful. It is similar to a blog 'bookmark' or 'favorites' list. The blogroll can become important in evaluating the interests of the blogger by the types of blogs he reads. A blogroll is a way of saying: If you enjoyed reading my blog, you might also enjoy reading these, because they are the ones I read. In other words, it is based on the birds-of-a-feather principle. (Create blogroll) Photos and videos can add a great deal of variety and information to a blog. Graphics are eye-catching and they allow you to personalize your blog and make it stand out. Photos can also be added to create a feeling and add depth to a story that you are writing on your blog. Your readers will be more likely to read your blog if it contains photos or videos.

LOCATING BLOGS

A number of search engines specialize strictly in locating information on blogs. The most common include blogsearch.google (http://blogsearch.google.com), Yahoo! Blog Search (http://www.ysearchblog.com), IceRocket (http://www.icerocket.com), SamePoint (http://samepoint.com/), and Technorati (http://technorati.com). Of all the blog search engines, Technorati is probably the most powerful. If you want to know, what people are saying and thinking about a topic, what they anticipate, what they love and hate, or what they think they understand — then the Technorati search engine is the one to use.

Dave Silfry launched Technorati June 2002. The service allows users to find the most relevant results on all media including blogs, photos, videos, and audio files. Using Technorati you can set up a Watchlist, which clips any blog postings that contain the search term(s) you specify.

Technorati is a convenient way to watch for discussions of a topic outside the sources you normally monitor. In addition to limiting a search to the Blog Directory, you can filter search results for posts with "a lot of authority," "some authority," or "a little authority." It calculates a blog's authority based on the number of blogs linking to that blog within the last six months. (Bates)

EVALUATING BLOGS

Regardless of whether you or your students become bloggers, blogs have probably already become sources of information about whatever topics you are interested in. Like Web sites, nearly everyone can post anything on a blog; therefore, blogs need to be evaluated carefully before quoting. Many of the same criteria used to evaluate Web sites for reliability can also be applied to blogs.

How does a user determine if a blog is a valid or reliable source for student or professional use? The first level of evaluation is by reading the blog in its entirety. Skimming the blog's last two months of archives provides a sense of the blogger's ideas and writing style.

Reading the blogs will provide a better overview than looking at their credentials. Next, follow the links, both in the posts themselves and the blogroll in the sidebar. If a blog approvingly links to other sources you know to be unreliable, you should consider the linking blog itself to be unreliable as well.

How will you know whether something you read on the web is true? You cannot know for sure. This makes it important to read carefully and to evaluate what you read. The first thing to remember is there are few authorities we can trust. In fact, authorities can lie as well, and people can impersonate authorities. Even if you trust the authority you are reading, you need to evaluate for yourself what they say. People do not always mean to mislead you, but they do.

You should depend on your own knowledge and judgment, and use this knowledge when you read blogs. This does not mean that you might not be wrong, but most people do not give themselves enough credit. Many are too quick to assume they must have been wrong if they read something different from what they suspect was the truth. Be sure to keep track of the contacts you have with certain bloggers. Learn to recognize whom to trust. When a blog says something, you need to ask yourself; have *they misled me before?* Blogs usually follow a pattern; sites that are trustworthy generally stay trustworthy, while sites that mislead you once will likely mislead you again.

Professionals are very careful about appearances. Governments and businesses especially take great care to manage their image. Individual people, too, try to cast themselves in the best light possible since people tend to trust those who look good. People create appearances in words as well. A flowery layout should not over-power the lack of content. The most important objective is to discover the facts. You need to check facts and ignore the appearances.

Remember that generalizations are often untrustworthy. People often generalize without thinking through the situation. Vague words might fool you into thinking that something is a fact, when it is actually a questionable generalization. In addition, question all statistics presented. Anyone can use statistics to mislead others to substantiate their point of view. Statistics must be based on scientifically gathered data.

When evaluating the validity of a blog, go to the source of the blog's statement or data and evaluate that source with the same criteria as you do on the original blog. Bloggers can write things about information and other people that may not be accurate. They might not have done this intentionally, but they could have misread or misunderstood the original document. Bloggers may also intentionally misrepresent the original or pretend that someone said something that they did not, so they can make the other person look bad.

CHOOSING BLOGGING SOFTWARE AND HOSTS

There are two primary ways of setting up a blog. The first is to use an online Web-based application such as Blogger (www.blogger.com), WordPress.com (www.wordpress.com), and Typepad (www.typepad.com) where the owner companies also serve as the host for their blogs. This is by far the easiest way to begin blogging, as it requires no technical skills and is very simple to set up and maintain.

Many of these blog services are free. Google now owns Blogger and will serve context sensitive ads on your free blog pages, but you can pay a modest amount to upgrade to an ad free version. WordPress.com is a free service while WordPress.org charges for their services. Wordpress.com's free blogging software and space is an ad free service, with rich and powerful tools. TypePad charge monthly fees and provides a great deal of flexibility.

A more complex, but more flexible, way of setting up your blog involves downloading blogging software and installing it on your own server or through your own contracted service. Such server maintained software includes Movable Type, (http://www.sixapart.com/movabletype) and Wordpress.org (http://wordpress.org).

The audience of the blog site needs to be taken into consideration. Some hosting sites such as LiveJournal (http://www.livejournal.com) and Xanga, (http://www.xanga.com) are more heavily used by a younger demographic and may be viewed as less 'professional' than the other services.

The popular Edublogs (http://edublogs.org) is based on WordPress technology and provides free blogs and wikis to educators. This site works well for e-portfolios, collaborative class work, online journaling, discussion, problem-based learning, or social constructivist learning.

EduBlogger (http://edublogger.org/) is an innovative teaching tool blending technology and pedagogy to assist teachers by integrating blogging, education, and teacher responsibilities.

EduBlogger is a fully featured blogging system that has many of the same features as any existing blog system, but it is structured specifically for classrooms. Using this blogging system, teachers can create assignments for students to complete. Responses to these assignments can be posted within the student's individual blog, which allows for greater student-to-student collaboration. With EduBlogger's extensive grading capability, teachers can grade student's responses to their assignment in a variety of ways.

David Warlick and the Landmark Project created a free classroom blogging system called ClassBlogMeister (http://classblogmeister.com) specifically for teachers and students. At this site, teacher can evaluate, comment on, and finally publish students' blog articles in a controlled environment.

Classroom teachers can set up a classroom blog and work in a sheltered environment designed to introduce K-12 students to writing for an authentic audience. BlogMeister combines blogging with the ability to approve posts before they are published. By using an approval system, teachers and media specialists can work with students to polish their work before they post it for public comment.

Another blog hosting service for teachers and students is November Learning (NL) (http://nlcommunities.com) that provides a safe and globally collaborative blogging environment. Using this site, teachers and students have the opportunity to create global connections across school curriculum. This service give students an opportunity to publish to an authentic audience, it enables teachers to share best practice with colleagues; and it enables families to access student assignments, student work, and important resources.

Gaggle Blogs (http://www.gaggle.net) are a way that students and educators can communicate with each other and the rest of the world. Gaggle Network is committed to providing teachers free filtered e-mail and blog accounts. Gaggle Blogs and e-mail are filtered for inappropriate words and phrases. All images are scanned for pornographic content and all URL links are checked for pornographic content. If any rules are violated, the offending blog entry will be blocked and sent to the author's administrator email address pending approval.

Gaggle offers two main types of accounts. The free accounts come with 2.5 MB of user storage space and are supported by advertisements. The paid version contains 75MB of storage space without advertisements along with several other features not found in the free version.

Microsoft has just released the Windows Live Writer (http://get.live.com/writer). This latest software makes it easier to compose compelling blog posts using Windows Live Spaces (http://home.services.spaces.live.com/) or your current blog service. Writer was designed to work with Windows Live Spaces (http://home.services.spaces.live.com) but it also is compatible with other weblogs including WordPress, TypePad, Blogger, LiveJournal, and many others.

The first thing to notice about Writer is that it enables true WYSIWYG (What You See Is What Your Get) blog authoring. You can author your post and know exactly what it will look like before you publish it. Writers can use pre-selected templates so that the styles of their blog such as headings, fonts, colors, background images, paragraph spacing, margins, and block quotes are consistent and enable users to edit their post using their preferred styles.

Windows Live Writer also includes other views such as HTML source-code editing, and web preview mode. You no longer have to waste time going through the process of publishing, refreshing, previewing, and tweaking your post to get it to look the way you want. It is all done within the program as you create your post.

Like most other blogging software, photo publishing into a blog is easy using Windows Live Writer. You can insert a photo into your post by browsing image thumbnails through the "Insert Picture" dialog or by copying and pasting copyright-cleared photos from a Web page. Once you have inserted the picture, Writer provides contextual editing tools to modify size, borders, text wrapping, and apply graphic effects. It also allows you to specify a smaller thumbnail that will link to a larger image for detailed viewing.

Using Windows Live Writer's map publishing feature you can insert a Windows Live Local map (http://maps.live.com) directly into a post. The view can be customized directly within Writer to show road, aerial or bird's eye detail and by adding pushpins. When readers click on the map, they get a larger view on the Windows Live Local site.

PROFESSIONAL USE OF BLOGS

Not every use of blogs in schools needs to involve classroom use. Blogs are a great way to communicate internally as well. School committees and groups that meet on a regular basis can use a blog to archive minutes of meetings, continue dialogues between meetings, share links to relevant information, and store documents and presentations for easy access later. Blogs are an excellent way to manage and communicate the knowledge that is created within the group.

Some school districts use blogs as articulation tools to showcase and share best practices, lesson plans, and *learning objects* such as worksheets or projects. A teacher no longer has to be in the same room to discuss what is and is not working in their classroom, but can work at their own pace at a more flexible time.

Blogs can be used as a building block for a school Web site. A major complaint about school Web sites is that few of them are updated on a regular basis. This can be corrected with a blog site. If each department had its own blog, they could make changes to their site as soon as needed without waiting for a webmaster to do it for them. If all the clubs and activities, all the sports teams, and all the student government bodies had their own site they could update it themselves without knowing complicated HTML coding. The overall school site would move from a static, *wait-for-the-Webmaster-to-update-it* type site to a *dynamic every-day-there's something-new on our Web site model.* (Richards 26)

Tim Lauer, principal of Meriwether Lewis Elementary in Portland, Oregon, uses a blog (http://lewiselementary.org) to post information, announcements, class projects, photos, and a calendar to communicate with the entire school community. He uses a separate blog to publish the staff bulletin and to encourage the staff to use the comment feature for discussions in order to build community.

Other schools are utilizing blogs to replace key sections of their Web sites. These blogs replace the school's home page; other times they are a prominent link from the home page. Blogs can be an excellent tool for a FAQ page, for ongoing updates about athletic and other extracurricular programs, and for reviews of past events. Blogs also can be used to replace teachers' classroom newsletters to parents and for internal communications to staff. (Solomon 126)

HOW TO WRITE MEANINGFUL BLOG ENTRIES

Maintaining an effective blog requires these basic considerations:

- A constant theme for your blog. This does not mean that you should write every blog posting about only one topic. Your blog should contain a variety of topics to keep people interested, but if the postings are disconnected, readers will quickly lose interest in reading them.
- A consistent voice. Choose the way you want to write your blog. Do you want it to be serious and down to earth, or funny? Consider tone. Do you want to use proper grammar all the time, or occasionally use slang? Be sure to add your own sense of style and personality to your blog.
- Honesty and sincerity. People will not read a blog that is written by someone who lacks credibility.
- Be informative and up to date. If you are attempting to create the impression that you are knowledgeable about a subject, be sure that you stay current.
- Differentiate between facts and opinions. If you are offering an opinion, be sure to qualify your post, making it clear that the content is intended as an editorial.
- Double check spelling, grammar, and punctuation. You will instantly lose credibility with your readers if you consistently misspell words.
- Select keyword-rich titles. If the goal of your blog is to increase your visibility, include related keywords in the title of the blog. Use the title as a headline to attract interest. Each item post should have a title that will attract attention but still be relevant to the post. The title should be no longer than 10-12 words.

- Update frequently. Create a schedule and stick to it. Realize that blogging requires time and effort, so do not create unrealistic expectations and then be unable to deliver. The more often you post, the better.
- Correctly maintained RSS feed will increase your blog's readership and distribution. (Refer to chapter two of this book for help in establishing RSS feeds.) Most blog audiences are small, but with time and regular updates, audiences grow. Bloggers may never have more than a few hundred readers, but the people who return regularly are generally interested in what you have to say.
- Select specific tags that best reflect the purpose of your blog. (Refer to chapter three of this book for ideas in choosing blog tags.)
- Select category labels that best describes the blog. The categories you select will determine the directory the blog will be located. If the blog ends in a wrong category, readers who are interested in that particular topic may miss it.

ADVANTAGES OF BLOGS IN THE CLASSROOM

One of the greatest advantages of integrating a web blog into the classroom is its ability to use RSS (really simple syndication) feeds. Educators and students can subscribe to an RSS feed and receive updates as they are published. They will be notified of new information or content without having to actually remember to revisit the Web page every few days.

Reading and creating blogs can teach critical reading and writing skills, thus leading to greater information management skills. Blogging can help students become more media and information literate by helping students clarify their choices about the content they write. Blogging also teaches students about how networks function, both human and computer, as well as helps teach the essential skill of collaboration. (Richards 38) Blogging can help pupils develop confidence, improve their self-expression, and achieve a sense of fulfillment from publishing their work since others can read their work besides the teacher.

Many skills and concepts need to be addressed when incorporating blogs into the curriculum. Blogging is not simply a matter of transferring classroom writing into digital spaces. All bloggers need to consider the difference between writing for a public audience as opposed to writing for a single person. Bloggers need to learn how to cite, hyperlink to other Web sites and when and why it is important to do that, as well as how to use the comment tool in educational ways.

EXAMPLES OF BLOGS IN THE CLASSROOM

Good Night, Mr. Tom blog (http://goodnightmistertom.blogspot.com) records the comments of a group of Year 7s (ages 11 and 12) in Auckland, New Zealand reading *Goodnight Mister Tom* by Michelle Magorian in their Literature Circles.

The kindergarten-grade 2 students and teachers developed *A Duck with a Blog* (http://duckdiaries.edublogs.org), which was a winner of the 2006 Edublog Award. This class shared their observations about a mother duck who has taken up residence on the school playground. The following year the same school developed their trout blog at (http://www.mcdsblogs.org/trout).

Anne Davis' ninth graders created the *Green Stream Blog* (http://itc.blogs.com/greenstream) to share information and explore how students can use blogging to improve their literacy skills.

"The Secret Life of Bees" (http://weblogs.hcrhs.k12.nj.us/bees) was created as a reader's guide by American Literature students at Hunterdon Central Regional High School. This blog provided an in-depth look into the book *The Secret Life of Bees* by Sue Monk Kidd. The exciting part of this blog is that the author of the book participated in the discussion and provided an in depth understanding of the story.

BLOG SAFETY

We have all heard the horror stories of death threats to fellow classmates, inappropriate pictures by young teens who are looking for dates, and illegal drug and alcohol use when students misuse blogs and other Internet sites. Because of the abuse on the public sites that are not closely monitored by teachers, some schools are blocking all access to any blogging sites. Too often, the technology itself is blamed for the problem and there is often little opportunity for pioneering teachers to provide adult role models.

Educators need the freedom to provide guidance and model the proper use of blogs for their students. Our young people will live in a world where they will have access to increasingly more powerful communications tools and it is the responsibility of the schools to teach them how to manage the power of these 21st century tools.

To protect their students while they learn to incorporate Web 2.0 tools into their curriculum and personal lives, there are a number of safeguards teachers and parents need to make.

1. Make sure the students never give out or record personal information on their blog.
2. Make sure students understand that their blog could be in a public space. If it is put on the Internet, odds are high that it will stay on the Internet, so they will want to write what they can be proud of for the world to view. (To avoid any problems a blog could be password protected.)
3. Remind students to never link to a site you have not read and agree with. Since it is impossible to police the Internet, when bloggers link to another site, they should be certain it is something with which they want to be associated.
4. Help students understand copyright issues and obtain a Creative Commons License or other copyright clearance whenever necessary.
5. Remind the students not to distort the content of copyrighted photos without disclosing what has been changed. Image enhancement is only acceptable for technical clarity.
6. Remind students not to show disrespect to anyone in their blog, whether it is a person, an organization, or just a general idea.
7. Remind students never to publish information they know is inaccurate -- and if publishing questionable information, make it clear it is in doubt.
8. Remind students to clarify what is opinion and what is fact.

SUMMARY

Moving from a read-only web to the read/write features of blogging is an exciting time for educators and the general public. Students can use this new technology to increase their reading and writing skills across the content areas as well as improve their collaboration and communication skills. Educators and parents have the responsibility to instruct their students in the safe and productive use of online tools in order to better prepare them for the 21st century job market.

Teachers, administrators, and business people are finding that blogs can become important tools in professional development, training, peer collaboration, sharing best practices, and communication with parents, customers, and stakeholders. Many schools and businesses are finding blogs a more effective way to communicate as well as more cost-effective then previous online methods.

Chapter 7

PODCASTING

WHAT IS A PODCAST?

Podcasting is a new word created by joining two words and their meaning – iPod and Broadcasting. Neither producing a podcast nor listening to one requires an iPod. The name came about simply because Apple Computer's iPod was the best-selling portable digital audio player when podcasting began. The power of podcasting is its ability to deliver content to any MP3 player, laptop, or desktop computer that is capable of synchronizing with Windows Media Player, Apple iTunes, or RealOne Player.

Podcasting is similar to a radio broadcast with the main differences being the transmission of pre-recorded content via the Internet versus a radio broadcast that requires a studio and a transmitter that sends out radio signals within a given area. Anyone who happens to be in the area can receive the radio signal with a radio tuned to the appropriate frequency. Podcasts, on the other hand, are audio programs that are stored as digital files on the Internet. These files can be retrieved from an Internet connection anywhere in the world.

Podcasting is a process of automatically receiving time-shifted audio or video from a personally selected subscription via a podcast-enabled RSS 2.0 feeds to a portable media device through the Internet. The podcast user is able to control what content they listen or view, and when and where they utilize it.

The podcast is a descendant of web logs, (or blogs) and is based on the same technology. The main differences between the two are the formats and delivery methods of the information. Blogs can be memos, articles, personal reviews, journals, or other forms of written content delivered on the web through a browser. The text in a blog may be accompanied by links and images or video and audio files. A podcast is an audio blog.

Subscribing to podcasts allows you to collect programs from a variety of sources for listening or viewing offline at whatever time and place you choose. In contrast, traditional broadcasting provides only one program at a time specified by the broadcaster. MP3 music and speech files have been available over the Internet for several years, but using RSS feeds, podcasting makes it simple for individuals to record and upload their own programs for users to subscribe to.

This ability to *aggregate* programs from multiple sources is a major part of the attraction of podcast listening. In addition, podcast producers have more flexibility since they do not have to satisfy advertisers nor do they have to worry about FCC regulations or pay attention to the corporate bottom line.

In a short period, podcasting has obtained the backing of educators at the elementary, secondary, and higher education level as a tool for the active, mobile learner. At the same time, business, political, informational, and recreational podcasts of all types abounded over the Internet. The main reason for the overnight success of the podcast is attributed to the millions of portable mp3 players with gigabytes of empty storage space being used by young people.

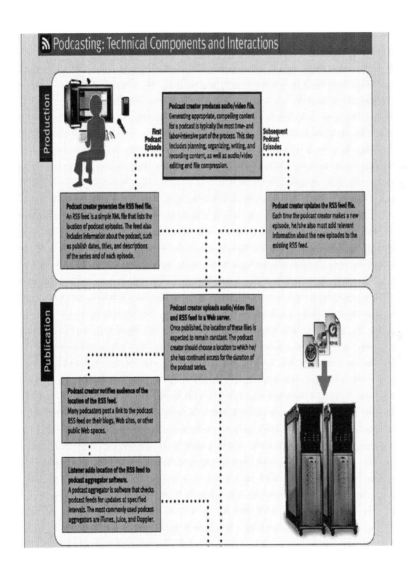

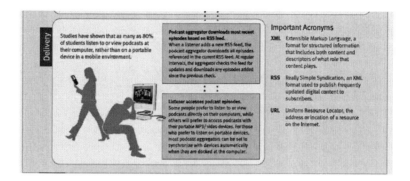

Figure 7:1 - Podcasting

http://connect.educause.edu/files/CMU_Podcasting_Jun07.pdf

(Used by permission: Ashley Deal, Office of Technology for Education & Eberly Center for Teaching Excellence, Carnegie Mellon University)

HISTORY OF PODCASTING

Former MTV video jockey Adam Curry and Dave Winer, the developer of the RSS 2.0 specification, are generally considered the *podfathers* of the podcasting community. In October of 2003, Winer and his friends organized the first BloggerCon conference at Harvard Law School's Berkman Center for the Internet and Society in Cambridge, Massachusetts. After much work, by September 2004, Adam Curry launched the podcasting concept, when he released a script that automatically downloaded audio files referenced in RSS files. The word about podcasting rapidly spread through the already-popular weblogs of Curry, Winer, and other early podcasters and podcast-listeners.

On October 11, 2004, the first phonetic search engine for podcasting, called Podkey, was launched to assist podcasters in connecting with each other. Then in May of that same year, the first book on podcasting, *Podcasting:*

the Do it Yourself Guide by Todd Cochrane, was released. In June 2005, Apple announced support for podcasts in its iTunes software, with distribution through its iTunes Music Store. Within two days, customers had subscribed to over 1 million podcasts from Apple's then-available 3,000 selections.

Podcasting has been instantly, if cautiously, recognized by *Big Media* for its potential; and most nationwide news programs are now available in podcast format. In some podcasts, paid advertisements are beginning to slip in. Mobilcast from Melodeo <http://mobilcast.com/> was one of the first attempts to provide podcasting to cell phones. Since then, other podcasting from a cell phone programs such as Gabcast (http://gabcast.com), Evoca (http://www.evoca.com), Gcast (http://www.gcast.com/) became popular. As soon as the price of cell phones with multi-Gigabytes hard drives comes down, the distinction between the cell phone and iPod will become blurred. (Handheld 70-71)

EDUCATIONAL USES OF PODCASTS

Podcasts are an excellent way to promote school activities. With podcasts, students and family members can enjoy guest speakers, concerts, competitions, and sporting events long after the event is over. Families are able to stay connected with their child's school activities if their work takes them away for extended periods. Minneapolis Public Schools was one of the first education organizations to offer broadcasts of school board meetings in audio or video format. (http://mplsk12mn.granicus.com/ViewPublisher.php?view_ id=2). If the parents of Highland Park Middle School students in Dallas, Texas miss a PTA meeting, they can

tune into the podcasts at
(http://hpms.hpisd.org/Parents/tabid/148/Default.aspx).

Many schools incorporate podcasts into the school district
Web site or an individual school's Web site using RSS
technology. These podcasts can deliver audio recordings of
daily news, press announcements, board meetings, or even
weather-related closings. Teachers can use daily or weekly
podcasts to summarize lessons for students and parents.

To begin integrating podcasts into the curriculum, teachers
often make a directory of podcasts that might be helpful for
student research. With the thousands of podcasts available
accompanied with limited time, it can be mind boggling for
educators to find the exact podcast to meet one's
educational needs. To retrieve a list of podcasts, users need
to use either a Podcast search engine or a Podcast directory
similar to the search engines or directories necessary for
Internet searches.

To broaden their research skills, older students may add
podcasts to these subject specific directories. However,
adult monitoring will be important since inappropriate
podcasts may appear in their search lists if open keyword
web searching is used.

Ways in which students can use podcasts within their
school environment include:

- Share information and research findings
- Debate issues and opposing viewpoints
- Share poetry or creative writing
- Review literature
- Apply topics and concepts to the world events
- Communicate in foreign languages" (Schmit 27)

Dave Warlick, a North Carolina educator, and the Landmark Project created The Education Podcast Network (EPN) (http://epnweb.org). This network is an effort to bring together, the wide range of podcast programming that may be helpful to teachers looking for content to teach with, and to explore issues of teaching and learning in the 21st century. Most of the producers of the programs listed on the EPN network are educators, who have found an opportunity where they can share their knowledge, insights, and passions for teaching and learning. A similar resource in the United Kingdom where students can produce and publish podcast is http://www.recap.ltd.uk/podcasting.

Two of the most popular podcast directories that cover all topics include Podcast Alley (http://www.podcastalley.com), which has the most extensive directory on the web, and the iTunes Podcast Directory (http://www.apple.com/itunes/store/podcasts.html) which is popular with iPod users.

Fall of 2005, Stanford University began a partnership with Apple iTunes Store to publish and host lectures called *Stanford on iTunes*. Within months, iTunes U. (for University) became a partnership between Apple and individual colleges and Universities for hosting and distributing audio and video lectures as podcasts, and vodcasts for their student bodies. Modeled after the Stanford on iTunes program, iTunes U. is a free service and allows a school to create an environment for instructors to upload their audio and video podcasts for distribution to their student bodies. Today scores of universities have thousands of hours of podcasts available for student use. For more information, consult http://www.apple.com/education/itunesu.

Audible.com, the popular source for online audio books is now providing Audible Podcasting (http://www.audible.com/adbl/site/audibleSearch/podcasts.jsp?BV_UseBVCookie=Yes). Audible listeners can receive all of their audio magazines, newspapers, and radio programs as podcasts in two different ways. Both methods require that users already have the appropriate software installed. The first method is to use a one-click subscription feature to add a personal podcast channel (RSS feed) to the podcast client. The second method is to "copy and paste" a URL to add a personal podcast channel (RSS feed) to a podcast client.

RETRIEVAL AND LISTENING TO PODCASTS

Once a desired podcast is located, in order to receive it, podcatcher software needs to be loaded on the computer. Podcatchers download podcast files by reading information contained in a RSS file, extracting different information from the same RSS file, and then displaying it on the software interface in human-readable format. Podcatchers allow people to scan and read a large number of Web sites without physically visiting the sites.

> **Podcatcher -** a tool that manages the selection and downloads of the podcast feeds automatically.

For details on setting up a podcatcher using RSS feed, refer back to chapter two. A list of podcatcher software and their location can be found in Appendix B.

Many podcasters have set up podcast-specific RSS feeds identifiable with white-on-orange icons. When a desired podcast is found, locate the links to the RSS feed necessary to add to your podcatcher application. To add the Web site's RSS feed, all one has to do is copy that URL and paste that information into the podcast-supported client's *Add Feed* window.

For iPod users, Apple has created a podcast directory of over 3,000 podcasts that can be accessed from their iTunes Music Store (http://www.apple.com/itunes/podcasts), allowing users to search by browsing through categorized lists. Podcasters can submit their shows via a link on the directory. Apple only links to the podcast files; it does not host them.

To receive a podcast, users need simply to click the 'Subscribe' button on the show's directory page, and it will automatically download to the user's iTunes library. Subscriptions are listed in a new podcast directory in the user's iTunes library, and new content is marked with a blue circle.

RESOURCES FOR PREPARING PODCASTS IN THE CLASSROOM

It has been said, "Give an educator a tool, and they will figure out a way to adapt it to the curriculum." When a creative teacher is provided with the necessary equipment, software, and resources to prepare a podcasts, he will soon develop ways to utilize podcasting to improve reading fluency, writing skills, and meet content area standards.

Not only do students listen to educational podcasts as consumers, but they also can produce their own. In the development of their own podcasts, students learn to research, plan, and write their scripts in advance, plus complete multiple audio takes before they're satisfied that the quality is good enough for broadcasting.

For several years, K12 Handhelds, Inc. (http://www.k12handhelds.com/podcasting) has led the way in providing schools with integrated solutions for mobile technology use in K-12 education. Soon after podcasting was developed, K12 Handhelds provided guidelines and resources for using and producing podcasting in the K-12 curriculum through numerous publications and web resources.

Learning Out Loud (http://www.learnoutloud.com) is a Podcast Directory containing free educational content that are selected to instruct, inspire, and enlighten the listener. It includes links to podcasts of tutorials from learning a foreign language to listening to classical literature.

Two recent books specific to podcasting in the classroom are *Kidcast: Podcasting in the Classroom* by Dan Schmit and *Educator's Podcast Guide* by Bard Williams. *Handheld Computers in Schools and Media Centers* by Ann Bell provides an overview of podcasting and other uses of iPods and other handheld devices within an educational environment.

LEGAL AND COPYRIGHT ISSUES IN PODCASTING

Unlike other forms of radio broadcasting, podcasts as they are broadcast today are not subject to direct censorship or regulatory control. This is part of its attraction; however, there are pitfalls for the naïve and unsuspecting. Just like any other form of published media, content on the Internet is subject to copyright, associated terms of use, and other laws such as defamation.

The laws covering copyright, offensive material, and libel are complex. Schools, like individuals, must take steps to ensure that their published podcasts do not infringe any existing copyright and that the content cannot be considered offensive or libelous.

One of the problems of the non-regulatory podcasts is that there are no controls against explicit content. Parents and educators need to engage young people in conversation about what that they are listening to, what they think about it, and how it applies (or does not apply) to their schoolwork or the development of their character.

Regardless of the local school policies, educators should always request permission and inform parents when students will be publishing their work online, whether it is text, photo, video, or a podcast. Parents should be assured that care is taken to protect their child's identity and that they will be supervised while online.

Portable digital recorders and cell phones allow podcasters to make their recordings anywhere. It is easy to record conversations without all the participants being aware that they were being taped. It is also possible to use software to record online conversations in audio chat programs such as Skype (http://www.skype.com), iChat (http://www.apple.com/macosx/features/ichat), or Gizmo (http://www.gizmoproject.com).

In most cases, it is unethical to secretly record conversations. If in doubt whether to tape or not, help can be found in *A Practical Guide to Taping Phone Calls and In-Person Conversations in the 50 States and D.C.* (http://www.rcfp.org/taping).

The use and exchange of music over the Internet has been one of the most complex issues users face. To use music in a podcast, creators have three options:

1. Arrange for music licenses that cover performance rights and royalties.
2. Use royalty free music (carefully check the conditions of use).
3. Create your own original music (you are then the copyright owner).

In seeking permission to use music that is protected under copyright laws, one first needs to determine who is the actual copyright owner of a musical work and how a license can be obtained to transmit a musical composition on the Internet. Generally, the songwriter and/or his or her music publisher are the owner of the rights to a musical composition. Licenses to perform a musical composition can be obtained from the organizations that represent a group of songwriters and publishers.

Locating the actual owner of a copyrighted work can sometimes be problematic since there are often a number of artist, editors, producers, or publishers involved. For assistance in locating copyright owners, consult government guidelines *How to Investigate the Copyright Status of a Work* at http://www.copyright.gov/circs/circ22.html. The Federal Copyright Office also provides a searchable database of

copyright owners since 1978 located at
http://cocatalog.loc.gov.

ASCAP (The American Society of Composers, Authors,
and Publishers) (http://ascap.com/weblicense) has worked
with many operators of Internet sites and services to
develop one of the best licensing solutions for the
expanding number of on-line music uses and business
models. Currently ASCAP provides two new versions of
their widely used Internet license agreements: "Non-
Interactive 5.0"
(http://ascap.com/weblicense/release5.0.pdf) for non-
interactive sites and services; and "Interactive 2.0"
(http://ascap.com/weblicense/release2.0.pdf) for interactive
sites and services.

Another popular Internet site to help users obtain copyright
permission on specific works is The Harry Fox Agency,
Inc. (http://www.harryfox.com) that provides a musical
copyright information source and licensing agency.
Schools, churches, community groups and other low-
volume producers of audio can quickly and easily obtain a
license online at
http://www.harryfox.com/public/songfile.jsp.
As an alternative to playing music controlled by the RIAA,
(Recording Industry Association of America) podcasters
can promote musicians who are not signed to a label and
are not members of the RIAA. Some music can legally be
played under a Creative Commons License
(http://creativecommons.org). Creative Commons makes
available licenses and tools to enable creators and licensors
to license their works on terms that are more flexible.

The Creative Commons license requires crediting the
artists and not pursuing commercial uses. Some of the

music licensed through Creative Commons is found on GarageBand (http://GarageBand.com). However, not all GarageBand.com artists have a Creative Commons License, and permission must be requested directly.

Royalty Free Podcast Music is available from numerous online sites. Such sites include the PodSafe Music Network (http://music.podshow.com) and Podsafe Audio (www.podsafeaudio.com). Both let independent musicians post free music podcasts and users must adhere to the Creative Commons license, which requires crediting the artists and not use the music for commercial gains.

The creator of a podcast is the copyright owner of that podcast. The words that a person speaks belong to them even if they are a minor. When they are published as a work, they are protected under copyright laws. By placing a copyright symbol and date on their work (or copyright element information within the RSS feed or MP3 files' ID3 tags, work can be properly attributed to the owner of the intellectual property. Just as students and adults are expected to respect the copyright laws of the music producers, so also the student's work should be respected for its copyright ownership. (Handheld Computer 73-74)

HARDWARE NEEDED TO PRODUCE A PODCAST

Any computer purchased within the last two years with at least a Gigabyte of memory, a fast processor, several Gigabytes of free space on the hard drive, and line in/out jacks should be capable of creating and receiving a podcast. A full featured USB or FireWire audio to digital converter provides more flexibility and higher quality sound. These devices work with higher quality XLR microphones and most will support two simultaneous microphones, making it easy to record a two-person interview. These devices also come with earphones to monitor the recording.

MICROPHONE

The microphone is probably the single most important component of a podcast setup. Microphone quality can range from a $10 microphone from Radio Shack to a professional grade. Microphone upgrades are the number-one purchase that will improve the quality of a podcast.

Types of microphones include the common dynamic microphones, which usually require no power source and the condenser microphone, which requires a phantom power (external power). If you choose a microphone that requires phantom power, you will want to make sure the mixer you buy has phantom power as well.

You might also consider adding a pop filter to your setup. A pop filter is a nylon mesh stretched over a small frame that is positioned between the speaker and the microphone. This helps eliminate the "pop" noise you hear when you speak words that contain explosive sounds (such as "p," "t" and "k").

HEADPHONES

Any full-cuff headset will enable podcasters hear the noise that is being introduced into the recordings and get a real sense of what is being recorded. A full line of headsets and headset reviews can be found at http://www.headphones.com.

Figure 7:2 - headphones

AUDIO MIXER

Figure 7:3 - Mixer

There is a wide difference in quality and price of audio mixers. The basic mixer needed by a podcaster starts at $49.95 but can top out as high as $500. Examples of possible mixers can be found at http://www.tapcoworld.com/products/index.html.

While basic podcasts can be produced without a mixer, the use of a mixer will provide these advantages:

1. Ease of manually controlling volume on background music via the mixer while talking rather than dealing with a mouse and trying to move a slide bar on a media player.
2. High quality, low-noise microphone amplifiers.
3. The capability to insert external audio and multiple microphone inputs.
4. The ability to record telephone interviews.
5. The capability to patch in special effects.

If telephone interview equipment is desired, simple telephone lines interface from Radio Shack known, as Smart Phone Recorder Control (http://www.radioshack.com/sm-smart-phone-recorder-control--pi-2123175.html), which costs less than $30, will work.

For additional features, JK Audio (http://jkaudio.com/inline-patch.htm) provides an Inline Patch for that can be used with talk shows when you may need access to audio from a working telephone. The unit's two back-to-back hybrids give complete control of audio from both sides of the call. An audio input jack lets users mix sound bites or music into the conversation. One stereo output jack provides the voice on one channel and the caller's voice on the other channel. A second output jack contains a mix of both voices.

BSW Professional Audio Gear (http://www.bswusa.com/podcastsolutions) has a wide selection of podcasting gear for those who are just starting out, those who want to upgrade their setup, and for those who strive for broadcast-quality Podcast.

PORTABLE MEDIA PLAYERS

While podcasts can be played on a desktop computer, to take full advantage of the mobile features of podcasting a portable media player is necessary. Any MP3 player or cell phone with a large hard drive can play a podcast. Mobile devices used for podcasting need to include the following features:

- Ability to synchronize with Windows Media Player, iTunes or other MP3 audio player.
- Recognizes a USB drive, preferably is USB 2.0 capable.
- Contains at least 256 MB storage space minimum with 512 MB or greater being best.
- Contains at least four hours of battery life.
- Ability to play other files other than MP3 is desirable.

- Wi-Fi (wireless ability to access the Internet) capability to synchronize podcasts and access other types of media content remotely is optimal.
- MP3 FM transmitter add-on lets users listen to their MP3 player via their car or home stereo is optimal.

SOFTWARE NEEDED TO PRODUCE A PODCAST

AUDIO EDITORS

To create a podcast, one first needs to create an MP3 (or similar) audio file using an audio editing software to edit the files and include music or sound effects.

Audacity (http://audacity.sourceforge.net) is a free, cross-platform, audio recorder and editor that is popular in the podcasting community. With Audacity users will be able to record live audio using their computer's sound input and then do simple editing to the recording and export it as an MP3 file. Due to copyright and patent restrictions, after installing *Audacity,* an MP3 encoder is needed for Audacity to be fully functional.

The LAMB (http://audacity.sourceforge.net/help/faq?s=install&item=lame-mp3) plug-in provides this functionality with just a few extra steps. In order for audacity to use this LAME encoder, it needs to know what the path to it is.

Recording in Audacity, or other audio editor such as GarageBand, is similar to recording on a tape recorder, but with more controls and visual information. When recording a podcast you may find it necessary to record the show in segments. Every time a new recording is started, another track is created. Several audio sources can be used in a podcast. A recording of a voice or voices, sound effects and music can be imported into Audacity. The sound levels of accompanying tracks can be changed over the course of the podcast and special effects can be after the narrative has been recorded.

Podcasts are generally recorded and posted in either mp3 or AAC format for the Apple. QuickTime 7 Pro on Mac OS X is an excellent program to record a podcast. To record the podcast users merely need to make sure the audio input device is connected, and go to 'File' then 'New Audio Recording,' Click the red 'Capture' button, begin recording, and then click the black 'Stop' button when finished recording. When finished, select 'Export' from the File menu.

To record a podcast with GarageBand you must create a Real Instrument track in GarageBand and adjust the Gain control on the audio interface to set the recording level of the speaker. Background music can be added in AIFF, MP3, or AAC file (except protected AAC files) format or a selection from GarageBand Apple Loops can be added. GarageBand Apple Loops allow the most flexibility since the length can be easily varied. Apple Loops helps you create your own unique copyright-free jingles for use in your podcast.

Other common audio editors for Windows Operating System includes QuickTime Pro (http://www.apple.com/quicktime/pro/win.html) for $29.00 and Adobe Audition 2.0 (http://www.adobe.com/products/audition/main.html) approximately $250.00.

Audio editors for the Mac Operating System include FinalCut Express (http://www.apple.com/finalcutexpress) for approximately $199.00 and FinalCut Pro (http://www.apple.com/finalcutstudio/finalcutpro) for approximately $1,299.00.

PODCAST GENERATOR

Once the audio has been edited, specific podcast software known as a podcast generator is necessary to publish the podcast for distribution. Apple's iTunes AAC format (http://www.apple.com/itunes/music) allows podcasters to create "enhanced podcasts" complete with embedded photos at publisher defined points throughout the podcast. These files are only compatible with iTunes and iPods, leaving many listeners unable to take advantage of this feature.

To create a Windows Media enhanced podcast, the producer needs an application that supports for Windows Media script editing. Several free and shareware RSS content generators such as RSS Content Generator 2.0. (http://pcwin.com/Software_Development/Easy_RSS_Cont ent_Generator/index.htm) are available to produce an RSS feed for a podcast. A list of software for publishing podcasts is listed in Appendix B of this book.

Once a podcast is complete, users will need a file transfer protocol (FTP) utility to upload the podcast to the web host. Many people use Internet Explorer to download files from FTP (File Transfer Protocol) sites and select software for download from tucows.com (http://tucows.com) or other free, or shareware download sites.

The final step in preparing a podcast is to select a hosting site. Some may choose to host their own podcast on their school's web server. Their hosting plans start at less than five dollars a month and provide a complete blogging package for podcasting with unlimited monthly bandwidth. Other podcast hosting sites are listed in Appendix B.

PLANNING A CLASSROOM PODCAST

The first step in planning a podcast is writing a brief objective for the podcast. In developing a podcast, it is critical to remain true to the objectives of the show. By defining a clear purpose, the rest of the planning becomes easier because the podcast now has direction and focus. One of the most important parts of defining a purpose is to identify the audience.

The objective should include the format, purpose, and audience for the podcast. Once the objectives are defined, students will need to decide what their main points will be, who will participate, what kind of script or outline they will need, and what kind of music will be appropriate.

After the planning segment comes the research and gathering of information and writing the script, identifying guests, Podsafe music, and a quiet location for recording. The content outline should be developed that includes general statements, bullets, or snippets of information about what to present and the order that you want to present it. This outline becomes what professional broadcasters call a *run-down*. (Williams 13)

SAMPLE RUN-DOWN FOR A SCHOOL NEWS PODCAST

0:00: Intro music
0:10: Introduce the announcers, the date, and location
0:20: Announcement of day's activities
1:00: Lunch menu
1:30: Interview of the football quarterback about the game that night
3:30: Explain the procedure and activities of the pep rally
4:30: Teaser or thought of the day
5:00: Interview with a biology class student after their field trip to the river
7:00: Invitation to the school play and short synopsis of the play
8:30: Congratulations to the students on the honor roll
9:00: Recap of events and sign-off
9:50: Exit music

After assembling all the components, the final step is to practice before the microphone. What works on paper, may not work as well when done orally. Even though students may be anxious to turn on the microphone, practice will help their comfort level and reduce the amount of extraneous hesitations in the final production. A polished recording can eliminate a great deal of work in the final editing phase.

RECORDING A PODCAST

When recording a podcast, care needs to be taken to reduce the noise. The brain filters out a great deal of noise to allow a person to concentrate on the more important sounds. However, microphones have no such filter, and podcasters may find that their recordings have picked up annoying noises in the environment. Two types of noise need to be addressed.

Environmental Noise – Surrounding noise.

Signal Noise – Mechanical noise between the microphone and the recording device.

Environmental noise is the most common form of noise in recordings. This noise usually comes from fans, air conditioners, refrigerators, fluorescent lighting, and street noise. If possible, a podcaster should power off as many appliances as possible. If that cannot be done, users might try recording in a closet with lots of clothes to muffle the sound, or to pull a blanket over themselves and their recording device.

The other type of noise is *signal noise,* which is the noise between the microphone and the recording device. With simple setups, signal noise can be caused by the use of an unshielded microphone cable. If possible, use XLR cables, which have an extra lead to avoid noise from interference. Remember to use the shortest possible microphone cables to cut down on signal noise.

In recording a podcast, proper microphone techniques are vital along with a good microphone. Proper microphone techniques are a blend of physical positioning, diction, speed, mouth form, presence, among others. The easiest problem to fix is microphone positioning. The speaker should be about a hand's width away from the microphone. In addition to the distance from the microphone, speakers can adjust their position relative to the microphone. Ideally, the microphone should be slightly above the speaker and to the left or right by up to 45 degrees.

Talking too fast is a common mistake for beginning podcasters. Therefore, it is advisable for the podcaster to practice the narrative several times before recording it. Another element of the speed problem is the tension of the speaker. Audio recording, with the presence of a microphone and hearing one's own voice through the headphones, is alien to most beginning podcasters and it is difficult to be relaxed while recording.
Another cause for stress is unrealistic expectations. No person should feel he could sound professional at the beginning. Podcasting is a learning, growing process. The successful podcasters are generally happy as long as each show sounded and felt better to them than the previous show.

EDITING THE PODCAST

After a podcast is recorded, the audio file needs to be loaded into the editing software for final production. At this point, background music can be added, the audio quality checked, any mistakes, noises, and filler words corrected, as well as weak areas re-recorded. The final step is to publish the MP3 file, generate an XML/RSS feed, check the MP3 link in the RSS feed, and publish the XML/RSS feed.

EVALUATING THE PODCAST

Before a podcast is distributed for public or semi-public listening, both teachers and viewers will want to evaluate the podcast. While specific details and expectations may vary, the general guidelines of a good podcast remain the same. A model for a class rubric to evaluate a podcast could look similar to the one in Appendix C.

HOSTING AND PUBLISHING A PODCAST

After the podcast is created in MP3 format, an RSS feed needs to be created with an RSS generator. The RSS generator gathers the necessary information for the RSS feeds channel and item elements. Options can be set along with the preferences that contain information about ownership, publishing settings, and audio compression. If the publishing preferences are set correctly, the software can publish the podcast and RSS feed by using the publish podcasts button.

RSS feed aggregators can be extremely finicky and sometimes the feed is not coded correctly. A simple missed bracket or a misspelling will cause the feed not to work properly and will not to be able to be downloaded. To solve this problem, after creating a feed, it needs to be uploaded to the server and then use an online validating tool such as Feed Validator (http://www.feedvalidator.org) to identify any problems. The feed validator will return a line-by-line analysis of any problems in the feed.

Adding an ID3 Tag to an audio file will ensure that the program is played. An ID3 tag is a file that is attached to an audio file containing album, artist, track, and other machine-readable information.

Figure 7:4 – ID3 Tag

If a podcaster has access to their own web server (or a shared server such as in a school), they can easily upload .mp3 content and an XML file that generates an RSS feed for podcasting clients. Using their own server, after they record their audio file, there will be two files to upload to the server, the audio file, and the XML file telling the subscribing listener's computer when there is new content and the nature of that new content. For those who do not have access to their own web server, the locations of popular online podcast hosting sites are listed in the appendix.

While publishing the podcast be sure to select specific tags that best reflect the purpose of your podcast. You may want to refer back to chapter three for ideas in choosing tags for each podcasts. At the same time, pay close attention to the category labels you select. The categories will determine the directory the podcast will be located. If the podcast ends in a wrong category, readers who are interested in that particular topic may miss it.

SUMMARY

Podcasting was first designed strictly for entertainment, but educators, business people, and activists in all interest areas soon learned to use this media as a tool to share content with possible listeners alongside professional broadcasters.

Chapter 8

VODCASTS AND SCREENCASTS

WHAT IS A VODCAST?

While the technology to play video on a handheld device has been available for several years, it was considered a novelty and few handheld users took advantage of this feature. However, within weeks of the release of the video iPod, news broadcasters, the television and film industries, educators, and amateur podcasters began releasing vodcasts for a wide variety of audiences.

Vodcasts use the same technology as blogs and podcasts except vodcasts includes video with its RSS feed. (See chapter two for RSS feed details.) Like blogs and podcasts, vodcasts depend on tags and categories to assist viewers in locating topics of interest. (For details on tags and folksonomy, see chapter three.)

To publish a finished video to the Web, there are literally hundreds of free options. YouTube (http://www.YouTube.com) and Google Video (http://video.google.com) attract tens of thousands of new videos every day. Video sites specifically for schools are available at TeacherTube (http://www.teachertubeonsite.com) and SchoolsTube, (http://www.schoolstube.com/). These services convert uploaded video into the Flash format and provide a URL link or HTML coding that can be embedded in a Web site or blog.

The drawback of these sites is that the length of a video is limited and the videos are in Flash format so users need a Flash player (http://get.adobe.com/flashplayer) to view, and they cannot download or save the videos. There are a number of digital video format converters that will change the flash video into a format that can be downloaded and played on a desktop computer or transferred to a handheld device.

Common YouTube video conversion programs include Zamzar.com (http://www.zamzar.com), Naevius YouTube Converter (http://www.naevius.com/youtube_converter.htm), and ConvertMyTube (http://www.convertmytube.com/). Conversion programs necessary to convert popular video formats to videos so that they can be viewed on an iPod include Quicktime Pro (http://www.apple.com/quicktime/pro), DVD to iPod Converter 5.0 (http://www.e-zsoft.com), and Videora iPod Converter (http://www.videora.com/en-us/Converter/iPod/).

Another disadvantage is that YouTube and Google Video and others like them do not specifically support Creative Commons (http://creativecommons.org) but many users are uploading files of CC licensed videos/music soundtracks to gain greater visibility. Ourmedia (http://ourmedia.org) is an open source solution for video producers and podcasters that offers free online storage and bandwidth through its partnership with the nonprofit Internet Archive (http://www.archive.org). Creative Common Licenses are available through Ourmedia.

Technically, videos posted on these sites cannot be classified as a vodcast unless an RSS feed is attached. Without the RSS feed, the viewer is not notified when a new video is posted, but must visit the host site and check for appropriate links to tags and keywords. The video remains on the YouTube video server and plays directly from the source without being downloaded onto the viewer's computer.

YouTube and Google Video do provide HTML coding for most videos that can be embedded into a blog that contains its own RSS feed. When the html coding is embedded in a blog, the subscribers to that particular blog will be notified through the blogs RSS feed that a material is available without distinguishing whether it is text, audio, or video.

SOURCES FOR EDUCATIONAL eVIDEOS AND VODCASTS

Discovery Education provides United Streaming (http://www.unitedstreaming.com) video-on-demand subscription service containing more than 1,000 copyright-cleared video clips to teachers and students for editing or reproduction in class projects. Students may use the content of United Streaming in a bona fide educational or research project.

Curriculum-on-Demand (http://www.digitalcurriculum.com) from Discovery Education is also a curriculum video-on-demand teaching and learning system that provides full-length educational videos and key concept video clips, audio, graphics, text, and images to subscribing teachers and students. According to their Terms of Use, these digital formats may be transferred to CD, DVD, or other physical media for student and teacher multimedia projects or student and teacher educational (and non-commercial) presentations only. This agreement broadens educational usefulness as it allows students to download videos onto handheld devices for viewing at their convenience.

TeacherTube (http://www.teachertube.com) was officially launched as a free service on March 6, 2007. Their goal is to provide an online community for sharing instructional videos and to provide a safe venue for teachers, schools, and home learners. It is a site to provide professional development with teachers teaching teachers, as well as a site where teachers can post videos designed for students to view in order to learn a concept or skill.

"With TeacherTube, community members can:
- Upload, tag and share videos worldwide
- Upload support files to attach your educational activities, assessments, lesson plans, notes, and other file formats to your video.
- Browse hundreds of videos uploaded by community members.
- Find, join and create video groups to connect with people who have similar interests.
- Customize the experience by subscribing to member videos, saving favorites, and creating playlists.
- Integrate TeacherTube videos on Web sites using video embeds or APIs.
- Make videos public or private - users can elect to broadcast their videos publicly or share them privately with those they invite." (About Us)

SchoolTube (http://www.schooltube.com) is another Internet video publisher for teachers and students who combine dynamic curriculum and community outreach programs. SchoolTube's mission is to educate and empower students and educators in safe, effective video production and online video sharing. Registered teachers must approve all videos uploaded on SchoolTube, which follow local school guidelines, and adhere to SchoolTube high standards.

SchoolTube has collaborated with The Student Television Network (STN) (http://www.studenttelevision.com/) to provide a nationwide network of broadcast journalism teachers and students who share their expertise with each other in an effort to create quality student videos of all types.

LearnOutLoud.com (http://www.learnoutloud.com) provides over 500 free audio and video titles. This directory features free audio books, lectures, speeches, sermons, interviews, and many other free audio and video resources. Most audio titles can be downloaded in digital formats such as MP3 and most video titles are available to stream online.

Google's video store (http://video.google.com) is less controlled than Apple's iTunes Music Store (http://www.apple.com/itunes/videos). Google prefers the term "the first open video marketplace." Google video allows anyone to post from the biggest TV network to the most talent-free camera-phone owner. Because of the possibility of inappropriate materials, parents and educators need to monitor the video downloads from the open sites.

The videos from iTunes Music Store cost two dollars an episode and every show is downloadable and transferable to an iPod. The video quality of color and clarity is good, often with professional production values, and there are no advertisements.

At Google's video store, some videos are copy-protected; others are not. Some can be downloaded, while others can only be viewed online. Only the copyright owner can upload to Google video store and if violations occur,

Google should be notified immediately. There is a wide variation of resolution and production quality at Google, and some videos include advertisements. Some videos are free, while others cost money.

One of the more popular exclusive audio/video search engine is AOL Video at (http://video.aol.com). AOL Video only indexes multimedia formats, including Windows Media, Real, QuickTime, and mp3s. Video search engines are available at Yahoo (http://video.search.yahoo.com). (Creating 88 - 90)

SELECTING SOFTWARE AND MEDIA PLAYERS

In recent months, consumers are turning from single function devices to all-in-one devices containing PDA/video/audio and sometimes even telephone features. The iPod Touch holds up to 40 hours of video depending on the size of the flash drive. This latest model of the iPod contains a 3.5-inch (diagonal) widescreen Multi-Touch display. The Apple Video Classic iPod can store up to 150 hours of video and can be viewed on a 2.5-inch color display.

Videos for the iPod can easily be downloaded directly from the iTunes Store for two dollars a program. Users can subscribe to and view some video podcasts with iPod-specific feeds. However, users cannot grab just any video podcast and drop it on an iPod. ITunes' inability to convert existing video into an iPod-friendly format is its biggest weakness. To make existing video into something that can be played on the iPod, you have to convert the video using either Apple's own $30 QuickTime Pro application or another video encoder that can work with the H.264 and MPEG-4 formats that iPod uses.

While Microsoft's Windows Media Player 10 and 11 automatically converts videos into a format suitable for watching on a Portable Media Player, third-party applications may be necessary to convert videos to a playable format for the iPod. The downside is that such applications are not prevalent and must be downloaded from the Internet. Format conversation is a cumbersome extra step to getting video into a portable media player. Windows Media Player can be used on all current Windows Desktop systems and on Windows Mobile Operating System for handheld devices.

DVDVideoSoft (http://www.dvdvideosoft.com/free-dvd-video-software.htm) provides a free video converter and multimedia software guides and tutorials. This site offers simple tools that let computer users produce a number of video activities. Some of the strengths of this site include the ability to download YouTube clips to a hard drive or the playback of YouTube clips on portable players, such as iPods, iPhones, PSPs (Play Station Portable) cell phones, or turning videos into MP3 songs or mobile phone ringtones with the Free YouTube to MP3 Converter.

FUNDAMENTALS OF DIGITAL COMPRESSION

Understanding digital compression is one of the most difficult, but also the most critical, aspect of digital editing for vodcasts. It is not necessary for the amateur video editor to memorize the ever changing complexity of digital compression, but a basic understanding of types and uses of compression will prevent a great deal of lost time and frustration. Knowing the type of compression that will be used in the final rendering of the video, will affect not only how the video is shot, but also how it is edited.

Uncompressed, a single minute of video totals about 1GB while a three-minute song would occupy about 27 MB of file storage space. Clearly, uncompressed audio or video is not an option. When the file is too large, you will need to use a compression (CODEC) program.

CODEC - a shortened form of compression/decompression.

The final step in preparing a digital video clip is called *rendering,* which compresses the video using some form of codec. All good video capture programs contain several compression options before recording or importing video.

Many video editing software programs will assist you in selecting suitable compression formats by organizing templates according to the output desired. The software will automatically limit frame size, frame rate, and audio quality and provide other space saving options. For example, if the user plans to distribute the movie as a CD, the user can simply choose one of the CD options and the software will adjust the necessary settings. (Creating 51)

Understanding the underlying principles of the compression settings will help the video producer achieve the quality of video desired. The following settings are available on most compression software:

- Quality Slider: Most compression formats provide a slider controlling general video quality, measured in percentage. Higher numbers result in larger file size and better quality. Default quality for most video compression is fifty percent.

- Data Type: Specifies video color bit depth, which determines the number of colors used. Normal video is 24-bit or 16 million colors. Reducing bit depth to 8-bit or 256 colors, decreases file size, but areas of complex color will appear smudged and blurred. Reduced bit depth is largely drawings or cartoons or contains large areas of flat color. Not all compression types allow the user to reduce color bit depth.

- Data Rate: Data rate is the amount of video information that is processed during each second of playback. Some compression schemes let the user specify an ideal data rate for a particular movie.

- Keyframe: Keyframes contain all of the information required to display the frame. All videos contain at least one key frame, which is the first frame of the file. After the first key frame, the software will automatically select other keyframes every time there is a sizeable change in content of the image. The compression scheme calculates and displays all colors in the Keyframe. In non-Keyframe frames, only the colors that have changed dramatically since the previous Keyframe are calculated. The remaining keyframes serve to improve the quality of the video, but they also increase file size. Generally, video producer should try using one keyframe for every ten seconds of video. (Creating 53-54)

SHOOTING COMPRESSION-FRIENDLY VIDEO

Shooting compression-friendly video is more difficult than shooting video that will be transferred directly to a DVD. The slogan to follow is "Mr. Rogers good, MTV bad." Detail and motion use the most bits in compressed video. The more complex the image and the more it moves, the more difficult it is for a codec to reproduce that image.

> **TIP:** When capturing video choose a compression setting that produces a better quality clip than needed. Users can always choose a lower quality compression setting when exporting the movie, but they cannot select a higher one.

Classic sedate video shooting and editing, compresses well, while jump cuts, wild motion graphics, and handheld shaky camera work are difficult to compress at lower data rates.

While shooting on-location the cameraperson must remain aware of what is happening in the background. Simple background elements help with compression while detail and motion should be avoided as much as possible.

If you plan to use text with your video, font selection needs to be made with care. The sharp edges and details of small text are difficult to compress, especially if the video will be reduced to a smaller resolution.

Rapid cutting of a video can cause problems. At each cut, the change in the video content requires a keyframe to account for the big change in the content. A cut every ten seconds is usually insignificant, but MTV-style editing, with a cut every second or less, can cause that section of video to be reduced to incomprehensible mush after encoding.

A cross-fade is one of the most difficult kinds of content to compress. The majority of methods that CODEC programs use do not work with blended frames of two different images. In these situations, each frame winds up a keyframe. It is much more efficient to use hard cuts. Fades to/from black are only slightly easier to compress than a cross-fade, and should be avoided, if possible. Wipes and pushes work quite well technically, but are not appropriate stylistically for many projects. A straight cut is often the best. (Creating 54-55)

PREPARING A VODCAST

Use close-ups and medium shots when shooting video for vodcasts.

Figure 8:1 - Vodcast

Preparing a Vodcast is a simple procedure using basic hardware and software available to the any consumer. For details on editing video for a vodcast consult *Creating Digital Video in Your School: How to Shoot, Edit Produce, Distribute and Incorporate Digital Media into the Curriculum* by Ann Bell and published by Linworth Publishing.

To create a vodcast from a video clip to be played on an iPod, the following steps need to be taken:

1. Create a movie. To reduce the size of the video, use the program's 'Export' command to save the movie in H.264 format.

2. Compress the movie in QuickTime Player Pro 7. Choose 'Export' from the 'File' menu and in the resulting 'Save Exported File As' dialog box, choose 'Movie to MPEG-4' from the Export pop-up menu. Click the 'Options' button and in the 'MP4 Export Settings' window that appears, choose 'MP4' from the 'File Format' pop-up menu. In the 'Video Format' pop-up menu, select 'H.264'. To keep file size smaller, select a modest image size (say 240 x 180) and a frame rate of 15 fps. Click the Audio tab and make sure that AAC-LC (Music) is selected in the Audio Format pop-up menu, then choose a modest data rate from that pop-up menu (48 kbps, for example). Click the Streaming tab and enable the Enable Streaming option. Last of all, click 'OK' to dismiss the window, and click 'Save' in the 'Save Exported File As' window to compress the video.

3. Upload the video onto a server. If a MAC user does not have access to a server, they can use an iDisk, which is a portion of .Mac (http://www.apple.com/dotmac).

4. Prepare an RSS feed by creating an XML file that will allow iTunes to access the movie.

5. Place the XML file in the same directory as the movie(s). If iDisk is used, place the XML file in the Sites folder.

6. Test the video in the browser by launching the browser and entering the address to the XML file in this form: http://www.yoursitename.com/yourvodcast.xml. A page should appear that lists the title of the vodcast at the top along with a Read More link that, when clicked, takes you to a page where you can view your movie. The URL in the Address field should have changed so that feed replaces http, as in: feed://www.yoursitename.com/yourvodcast.

7. Check the Vodcast in iTunes by Launching iTunes and selecting "Subscribe to Podcast" from the "Advanced" menu. Enter the desired URL and then click 'OK', an entry for the vodcast will appear in the Podcast playlist within iTunes' main window and the video will begin downloading to the computer.

8. Let the world know that the vodcast is available and instruct them to enter that URL in the Subscribe to Podcasts window to view the work. The video will appear in the viewer's iTunes' Podcasts area. (Breen)

Another quick and easy tool for publishing audio and video podcasts with the MAC OS is VODcaster (http://www.twocanoes.com/vodcaster). VODcaster allows users to enter the important information without having to know XML.

Most video-editing software package can be used to create a video for a vodcast, but one software in particular, was created strictly for vodcasting. Vlog It (http://www.adobe.com/products/vlogit) software from Adobe lets users create newscast-like blog entries via a simple, drag-and-drop interface. Users can insert music or video clips into a vertically scrolling timeline, and then use a camcorder or Webcam to record their video and a microphone to add voiceover.

The Vlog It timeline has an integrated teleprompter for displaying the narration. If a user has a green background, they can use composites to add a video or animated backdrop of their choice with a chromakey effect similar to what weatherpersons do. Once the video blog is created, the software automatically adjusts the compression and codec settings based on the selected output choice. Vlog It can even upload the file to a video-hosting service.

INCORPORATING VODCASTS INTO THE CURRICULUM

The web's shift from a tool of reference to one of collaboration presents teachers with rich opportunities for e-learning. Some of the ways vodcasts can be used in schools include:

- Creating a short introduction to your school, or the course you teach, for potential students and parents
- Using vodcasts for professional development
- Student produced digital story telling
- Developing a collection of teacher created subject specific videos
- Recording lessons for students and parents to access in their own time.
- Recording discussions ("talking heads") as a course resource
- Including vodcasts as part of a student's e-portfolio
- Locating and using videos on current issues, a natural disaster, or a controversial event as part of project research materials

- Enabling students to do a video presentation instead of a PowerPoint

- Enabling students to submit work in the form of vodcasts
- Enabling students to use foreign language vodcasts to improve linguistic skills
- Using vodcasts to get an insight into another country's culture, or another person's daily lifestyle
- Enabling students to create a vodcast of a school field trip
- Enabling students to create a personal vodcast such as "My summer vacation"
- Asking students to create a vodcast to meet a real need, as part of a coursework project, such as for use by a local business, or application for music or sports college admission.

SCREENCAST

Screencasts are much like vodcasts in the fact they are short video clips. However, vodcasts are videos taken with a

video camera or still photos assembled as a slide show. Screencasting is capturing what is happening on a computer screen, also known as a *video screen capture,* and adding an audio narration to it.

Graphic 8:2 - Screencast

Screencasts are designed to educate, entertain, or influence an audience. Screencasting is an effective mean to humanize the content used in e-learning by combining video, text and audio onto the screen at the same time. Presenting materials in this fashion makes lessons more accessible to a variety of learning styles and are more engaging to the learner.

Since the final product of a screencast is the same as a vodcasts, the publishing steps are the same. The final screencasts can be saved in video formats (.mp4, .avi, .wmv, .mov) and uploaded to a free service such as YouTube or Google Video so they can be embedded into Web pages or blog sites simply by pasting a code. A RSS feed generator can be used to notify subscribers that another screencast is available.

Like blogs, podcasts, and vodcasts, users need to take care in selecting tags and categories. Well-chosen tags lead to the greatest exposure and fit within a tag cloud and folksonomy.

CREATING SCREENCASTS

Four basic steps in creating a screencast include:

1. Capturing what is on the screen
2. Producing the audio
3. Combining audio and screencast
4. Publishing the file to the Web

To create a screencast you need screen-recording software, capable of capturing in real-time the mouse movements, clicks, and screen activities. Some software includes the ability to record audio while capturing the activity on the screen, and not in a second-pass session to add the audio.

It is recommended to use fixed width to capture and auto pan when creating a screencast. Autopan means the region you are recording moves as you move the mouse. This permits the text on the screen to be easier to read than if you had recorded the entire desktop. For most situations, when creating a screencast it is best to use a fixed region (640 wide by 480 high).

NARRATED PRESENTATIONS AND SCREENCAST SOFTWARE

Narration and music can be added to PowerPoint to create a narrated presentation that will appear exactly like a vodcasts or screencast except that a PowerPoint slide or graphic is viewed on the screen. Several powerful software programs are available to help users prepare screencasts or create and share narrated multimedia presentations for online sharing and podcasting.

Jing (http://www.jingproject.com), a TechSmith product, is an always-ready program that instantly captures and shares images and video from a local computer to anywhere. Users receive up to 2GB of screenshot and screencast storage and 2GB of transfer per month on Screencast.com. This program is an excellent cross-platform tool to quickly create and share screenshots or screencasts. Anything made with Jing can automatically be saved to Screencast.com, a local folder or network drive, an FTP server, or even Flickr.

Windows Media Encoder (http://www.microsoft.com/windows/windowsmedia/forpros/encoder/default.mspx) and a microphone are all that is needed to create a screencast in the Windows environment. This software is a powerful tool for educators and students who want to capture audio and video content with Windows Media.

On the MAC side there is an inexpensive option of Snapz Pro (http://www.macupdate.com/info.php/id/6149). For more ambitious efforts that require more precise editing or capturing, you will need a commercial program such as Camtasia Studio (http://www.techsmith.com/camtasia.asp).

ProfCast for MACS < http://www.profcast.com/ > is an inexpensive ($59.95) Macintosh program that allows you to directly record audio narration with a PowerPoint or Keynote presentation and post it to the web as an enhanced podcast. It provides a low cost solution for recording and distributing lectures, special events, and presentations as vodcasts. ProfCast will capture all the elements of a presentation, including slide timings, bullet point builds, and voice narration and allow users to record the presentation as they give it. ProfCast also helps users publish their recorded presentation as a vodcast, complete with RSS.

On the Windows side, one of the most robust tools for creating online narrated PowerPoint presentations is Articulate Presenter (http://www.articulate.com/products/presenter.php). Articulate Presenter lets non-technical users create e-learning presentations by adding narration and interactivity to a standard PowerPoint file. With Articulate Presenter, the PowerPoint content is converted to Flash, which is already installed in 98% of Web browsers. Conversion to Flash reduces the size of the presentations so they download fast and effectively.

On the powerful side, Camtasia Studio (http://www.techsmith.com/camtasia.asp) also lets you create narrated PowerPoint presentations for online sharing. A number of less robust shareware PowerPoint to flash converters are also on the web for download. Care needs to be taken as to the comparison of features versus cost.

EDUCATIONAL USES OF SCREENCASTS

Some of the ways screencasts are used within a school environment include:

- Tutorials – A popular site of online screencast tutorials for most software packages is Atomic Learning (http://movies.atomiclearning.com).
- Software Reviews
- Animated whiteboard demonstrations
- Spontaneous teacher-produced demonstrations
- Short how-to videos
- Video handouts
- Using Sketchcast (http://sketchcast.com) to explain math concepts. SketchCast is a Web site that allows users to create sketches with recorded voice. After signing up for the free, users can start drawing their sketches then record their own voice to explain what they are doing. When they are finished, they can embed a video player on any Web site to display the sketches.
- Add narration to a PowerPoint Presentation and save it as a screencast.

Some teachers like to convert their screencast for use on a variety of portable media devices and then store them on the school web server or upload to an online video storage site for later download to a mobile device.

SUMMARY

Preparing educational videos and sharing them over the Internet has been popular for a number of years. Now, with the advent of Web 2.0 tools and mobile devices with the capacity to play video, the potential for both the advanced and novice user to share video is exploding at all educational, informational, interest, and recreational levels. Their potential is limitless.

Basic digital videos can not only be e-mailed or posted on a Web site, but can be broadcast to subscribers using RSS feeds whenever a new program becomes available. Since vodcasts can be produced by all levels of equipment, from the very basic consumer level, to the professional level, amateur vodcasters can easily find hardware and software that meet their needs.

Chapter 9

WIKIS

INFORMATION LITERACY

Information literacy and communication is not a matter of knowing what source to use, but of being able to decide what source to use, based on the goal at hand. Therefore, we need to understand the entire arsenal of Web 2.0 tools that are available in the World Wide Web. Using a wiki is a valuable collaborative tool to use in information searching and production.

> **"...The best thing we can teach our children is how to teach themselves."** (Intellectual 11)

WHAT IS A WIKI?

Wiki is a Hawaiian term meaning "fast." The first such software to be called a wiki or WikiWikiWeb was named by Ward Cunningham in 1995. A Wiki is a combination of a Web site and a Word document. At its simplest form, it can be read like any other Web site, with no access privileges necessary, but its real power lies in the fact that groups can work collaboratively on the content of the site using nothing but a standard web browser. Wikis help us capture a community's knowledge and collect it into a manageable format, making it accessible to everyone.

Wikis are Web sites that anybody can edit, if the moderator desires. However, many choose to make their wiki private or semiprivate using a password. You can tell a Web site is a wiki by the "edit" tabs at the top of the page. Wikis are easy to use so you can create or edit the actual site contents without any special technical knowledge or tools.

Graphic 9:1 Wiki

The data entered into a wiki is maintained in a separate database from the program files. Because of this feature, a wiki has the ability to keep track of the history of a document as it is revised. Each time a person makes changes to a wiki page, that revision of the content becomes the current version, and an older version is stored. Versions of the document can be compared side-by-side, and edits can be necessary.

HOW WIKIS WORK

Since a Wiki works as a combination of a Word document and a Web site, if something is missing or incorrect in a wiki and permissions are allowed, you can easily add information or ideas to make changes to that wiki. People who contribute to a wiki understand that others may also delete or change their entries. The knowledge of the group is greater than the knowledge of an individual, and the end product of a wiki is the result of the group's interactions. The process actually becomes the product.

Collaboration and collective efforts are often confused, but they are not similar and they are two distinctly different efforts. Collaboration is people working together (often with a common goal) to build one thing, such as a wiki page with one understanding. Collective efforts are the aggregation of people's individual efforts, sometimes in the same service, but do not have a common goal or common effort. Social bookmarking sites such as delicious (http://delicious.com/) are the combined, collective understanding of individuals tagging of those Web pages for the use of all participants. (Vander Wal)

Wikis have two modes, *read* and *edit*. The default mode is the *read state,* which means that the wiki page looks just like a normal Web page only with an edit tab at the top. If you want to edit the wiki page, you must access the wikis *edit mode.* To edit a wiki, you point your Internet browser to the wiki URL and click an edit button or link entitled 'edit this page' featured on each wiki page.

Incorporating wikis into the curriculum promotes a constructionist style of learning in which learners build new ideas or concepts on their current/past knowledge and in response to the instructional situation. It implies the notion that learners do not passively absorb information but construct it themselves.

Each wiki contains a page history tab. Each time someone edits a page, it takes a visual snapshot of the changes so users can see in a glance how much has changed. Was it one line or the entire page? Users can also compare any two versions of a page by clicking "select for comparison" on one version of a page and then "compare to selected" on another. Wiki software will keep every version of every page and make it easy for authorized members to revert to a previous copy, if necessary. The wiki history can be used to track wiki use and collaboration.

Each wiki also has a discussion area to keep the discussions separate from the wiki itself. You can plan and discuss on this page before posting to the wiki for public viewing.

DIFFERENCES BETWEEN A WIKI AND A BLOG

Blogs are designed for one-to-many communication. A blog shares writing and multimedia content in the form of "posts" (starting point entries) and "comments" (responses to the posts). While commenting, and even posting, are open to the members of the blog or to the public, no one is able to change a comment or post made by another. The owner of the blog is able to delete undesirable comments. The usual format is post-comment-comment-comment, and so on. For this reason, blogs are often the vehicle of choice to express individual opinions or explain a specific piece of information.

A wiki has a far more open structure than a blog and allows others to change what another person has written. This openness trumps individual opinion with group consensus. Unlike blogs, wikis have a history function, which allows previous versions to be examined, and a rollback function, which restores previous versions.

DIFFERENCES BETWEEN A WIKI AND A FORUM (DISCUSSION BOARD)

Forums (Discussion Boards) are excellent tools for letting many users ask questions and letting many people answer. Although a discussion forum can contain links, it tends to have a rather linear appearance: someone posts a message, then someone else responds, then the first person reacts to that, and so on. The discussion forum does not have the immediacy of a "big picture" view that the wiki does. The emphasis of a discussion board is on conversation as compared to product building.

Wikis are excellent for collaboration. If you want to let others collaborate, add files, suggest links, and create a document that is comprehensive and up-to-date, use a wiki format. If you would like to have others discuss an idea or issue, a discussion board would best meet your needs.

WIKINOMICS

The new art and science of wikinomics is based on four powerful new ideas: openness, peering, sharing, and acting globally. (Tapscott 20) Participants in peer production communities have many different motivations for contributing to a project, from fun and altruism to achieving something that is of direct value to them. Though consensus is the general rule, most peer networks have an underlying structure, where some people have more authority and influence than others have.

Peer production is emerging as an alternative model of production that can harness human skill, ingenuity, and intelligence more efficiently and effectively than traditional firms can. (Tapscott 66) Peering succeeds because it leverages self-organization -- a style of production that work more effectively in certain tasks than hierarchical management. (Tapscott 25) The rapid scientific and technological advances are among the key reasons why this new openness is surfacing as a new imperative for managers. (Tapscott 21) Wikipedia is an example of peer production, a new way of producing goods and services that harnesses the power of mass collaboration. (Tapscott 65)

WIKIPEDIA

Wikipedia is an open-source encyclopedia that lets anyone create or edit an article. It is the largest encyclopedia in the world, offered free of charge. Jimmy Wales created Wikipedia in 2001 on the premise that collaboration among users will improve content over time, in the way that the open source community steadily improved Linus Torvalds' first version of Linux. (Tapscott 71) As of January 2009, volunteers around the world have written 12 million articles (2.6 million in English) collaboratively, and almost all of its articles can be edited by anyone who can access the Wikipedia Web site. (http://en.wikipedia.org/wiki/Wikipedia)

> Imagine a world in which every single person on the planet is given free access to the sum of all human knowledge. That's what we're doing.
>
> (<http://en.wikiquote.org/wiki/Jimmy_Wales>)

Since anyone can make changes to it, Wikipedia often receives criticism concerning its accuracy, especially when compared to print encyclopedias. In 2005, *Nature: an International Journal of Science* conducted a comparison study between Wikipedia and the Encyclopedia Britannica. The conclusion of that study was that there were 2.92 mistakes per article for Britannica compared to 3.86 for Wikipedia and that Wikipedia is about as good a source of accurate information as Britannica. (Terdiman)

Since *Nature* released their study, an active debate intensified as to the value of Wikipedia. Those defending the online, open-source encyclopedia maintain that even though incorrect information can be posted, there are vastly more editors who want to get Wikipedia right than want to make it wrong. Each Wikipedia article has been edited an average of twenty times, and for newer entries, that number is higher. (Tapscott 72) Wikipedia is up-to-dated more frequently than Britannica and errors are corrected as soon as they are detected without waiting for the next print update as is necessary with print encyclopedias. Wikipedia is peer-reviewed by the world community with more than one cultural viewpoint.

Those that question the validity of Wikipedia point to the fact children and those wishing to create mischief can amend and contribute to the knowledgebase. Someone who does not have full knowledge of the subject can amend expert-written articles. Contentious opinions and inaccuracies can be published as facts until someone identifies them and makes appropriate changes.

Wikipedia does not claim to be perfect and admits that it does contain inaccurate information that has not yet been discovered to be wrong. They encourage readers to question and verify the information somewhere else — just like you should with all sources. In general, popular articles are more accurate because they are read more often and therefore any errors are corrected in a more timely fashion.

Wikipedia is developing rapidly, so the reliability of the encyclopedia is improving daily. Because readers continually compare articles to what they already know, articles tend to become more accurate and detailed. Certain articles about many of the major sciences were developed from other free or public domain journals, books, or encyclopedias. This provides a reliable basis upon which encyclopedia writers can develop information that is more current.

WIKIPEDIA SELECTION FOR SCHOOLS

The concern of having young children accessing Open Source material on the Internet has caused some groups to take an alternative action from filtering Wikipedia in its entirety. SOS Children (the world's largest orphan charity) of the United Kingdom and the Wikimedia Foundation have launched the Wikipedia Selection for Schools. This DVD contains the content of a fifteen-volume encyclopedia - with 24,000 pictures, 14 million words, and articles on 4,625 topics. It includes the best of Wikipedia, and many thousands of pages of extra material specifically selected to be of interest to children ages 8-17 who follow the UK National Curriculum and similar curricula elsewhere in the world. (SOS)

WIKIBOOKS

Wikibooks (http://wikibooks.org/) is a collection of open-content textbooks, which include textbooks, annotated texts, instructional guides, and manuals. As a rule, only instructional books are suitable for inclusion, while all other types of books, both fiction and non-fiction, are not allowed.

Wikibooks can be used in a traditional classroom, an accredited or respected institution, a home-school environment, or for self-learning. Some in education think a project like Wikibooks gives academics new outlets for their research and puts a great deal of pressure on traditional textbook publishers to adapt to new technologies. Wikibooks' choice of license ensures that books will remain freely distributable forever.

The hope of its founders is that by turning the Wikibooks keys over to a worldwide community of writers and editors, the project will eventually contain tens of thousands of books and smaller entries on a wide range of topics. In each case, the idea is that any Wikibooks reader could create his or her own book or make edits to an existing title.

Wikibooks is not for original research or a place to pose theories or solutions. If you have done primary research on a topic, it is best to publish your results in normal peer-reviewed journals, or elsewhere on the Web, such as at the Academic Publishing Wiki or Wikiversity. Wikibooks is not a place to publish original works. Wikibooks is also not a repository of public domain source texts, which is the purpose of their sister project Wikisource (http://en.wikisource.org/). (Wikibooks).

WIKISOURCE

Wikisource (http://en.wikisource.org/) is a free library of source texts which are in the public domain or legally available for free redistribution. Wikisource is an official project of the Wikimedia Foundation and a sister project of

Wikipedia and Wikibooks. It began in November 2003, as a collection of supporting texts for articles in Wikipedia.

The difference between Wikibooks and Wikisource is that Wikisource focuses on material published elsewhere. *Wikisource* can be viewed as a library of public domain works. Wikibooks are instructional materials written by the contributors themselves. The area of annotations to source texts is a gray area, with some legitimate overlap between the two.

While Wikipedia is an encyclopedia, Wikisource is a library. Wikipedia contains articles *about* books; Wikisource includes the book *itself*. To some extent, both may include bibliographical material about the author.

WIKIVERSITY

The English language Wikiversity Web site opened August 15, 2006 as a collection of learning materials and activities that are being collaboratively developed in wiki format. Wikiversity hosts and develops free learning materials for all age groups. It excludes online-courses, while it is based on *learning by doing*, or *experiential learning*.

Wikiversity will be a radically different kind of learning platform/environment/resource and its students and its practitioners will continually shape its identity and scope. Wikiversity does not yet certify student's mastery since there is no way of assuring who is doing the work for a course. They attempt to teach the same material many accredited schools do, and to teach the material as well but there is no guarantee they will gain accreditation in the future. Wikiversity's goal is to teach the material to whoever wants to learn it, to the best of our ability and theirs. (Wikiversity)

FREE HIGH SCHOOL SCIENCE TEXT (FHSST)

FHSST (Free High School Science Texts) (http://www.fhsst.org/) is a project that aims to provide free science and mathematics textbooks for Grades 10 to 12 science learners in South Africa. Young South African scientists initiated the project. It now brings together scientists from around the world who are willing to contribute to the writing of the books included in the project.

Its goal is to provide complete, free high school science textbooks and resources that can be used free of charge anywhere else in the world. Both students and teachers can use these free resources alone or in conjunction with other education initiatives in South Africa which adheres to the South African school curriculum and the outcomes-based education system.

WIKI AS A COLLEGE TEXTBOOK

A wiki has become a primary learning tool, replacing textbooks and allowing for improved collaboration among students in at least one Boston College classroom. Gerald Kane, assistant professor of information systems at the Chestnut Hill, Massachusetts school, has been using a wiki from SocialText Inc. (http://www.socialtext.com/) as the primary teaching tool in his classrooms since October 2006. His classes rely on this technology to integrate content from other Web 2.0 technologies like social bookmarking tools, RSS systems, and Google for his "Computers in Management" courses (Havenstein).

SELECTING WIKI TOOLS

Features to consider when selecting wiki software include:
1. Ease of Use - The ideal wiki tool should be learned in a matter of minutes.
2. Appearance – Clean and neat so users can find contents easily within the wiki.
3. Cost - There are many free wiki tools on the web.
4. Security – The wiki creator should be able to protect certain pages from changes and be able to set members and permissions, and determine who can view the wiki.

TYPES OF WIKIS

Three types of wiki software may be relevant to you. You can install the software yourself on a server or a desktop, or select Web sites that host wikis for you.

HOSTED WIKIS

Hosted wikis, often referred to as wikifarms, offer open and/or password protected wikis with different levels of customization and extendibility. Some of these wiki farms are free; others offer paid features. A few examples include:
- PeanutButterWiki (http://pbwiki.com/). This site claims that creating a wiki is as easy as making a peanut butter sandwich. PBWiki supports itself through Google AdWords.
- Wikispaces (http://www.wikispaces.com/) Wikispaces offers advertising free wikis for educators.
- SeedWiki (http://seedwiki.com/).

SERVER-SIDE WIKIS

MediaWiki (http://www.mediawiki.org/) is a free wiki software package originally written for Wikipedi that must be installed on a web server. MediaWiki is licensed under the GNU General Public License (GPL). It is designed to be run on a large server farm for a Web site that gets millions of hits per day.

DESKTOP WIKIS

Desktop Wiki software can be installed on a local computer and does not require a web server for administration. It works for the end user and is not shareable on the web.

Examples of desktop wikis include:
- VoodooPad (Mac OS X) (http://flyingmeat.com/voodoopad/)
- WikidPad (Windows) (http://wikidpad.sourceforge.net/)
- Instiki (Windows and Mac) (http://instiki.org/)

BENEFITS AND USES OF WIKIS IN SCHOOL COMMUNICATION

Wikis can be used for board, school, and classroom communication for families, classrooms, sports teams, community groups, and book clubs. Educators can create a glossary of terms for specific subject areas. Some schools have their students research information about the past, present, and future of their school to add to the school wiki. These wikis could include pictures and text.

Faculty can use the wiki format to collaboratively author lesson plans and curriculum necessary to help students meet their educational standards. Faculty and administrators can save time and energy by producing policies on wiki software.

School teacher/librarians can produce pathfinders in a wiki format. These pathfinders can lead researchers through information jungles by suggesting keywords, tags, and call numbers along with books and journals to browse. These wiki pathfinders can link researchers to critical readings, Web sites, blogs, wikis, portals, and databases. They can suggest strategies for searching and for documentation. The pathfinders can host teacher presentations, handouts, rubrics, and organizers, as well as models of student work. (Valenza)

BENEFITS AND USES OF WIKIS IN THE CLASSROOM

Traditionally students write papers that only their teachers will read. When students know their peers will read what they write, they take more care and they try harder. When educators incorporate a wiki into the curriculum, their students get a gentle introduction into online collaboration, and they will remain engaged beyond the classroom. A wiki can help teachers capture the students' combined knowledge and present it in a manageable way, making it accessible to everyone.

Students can use a wiki to share research and data while working on a group project as will was writing a 'choose your own path' story. In addition to students reading existing wikis on topics of interest, the implications for education include group collaboration and problem solving, peer editing during the writing process, and electronic portfolios. Students can work from anywhere, which means they are able to contribute on their own schedule rather than being limited to the school day or class period. Wikis keep track of changes, so teachers can look at successive versions of documents for electronic portfolios or the contributions each student has made. When the work is complete, students can invite parents and others to read their work and comment. (Solomon 57-58)

SAFETY GUIDELINES IN USING A WIKI

Many schools may need to upgrade their Acceptable Use Guidelines to incorporate the use of wikis within the classroom. Some district filtering prevents access to the wiki tools from school. If this happens to you, ask your administrator to facilitate the unblocking of the wiki's exact URL.

In general, a district wiki policy should cover issues related to student identity on the World Wide Web, in order to prevent students from including specific identifying information in classroom wikis, such as full names, photos and emails. A district wiki policy should also include guidelines for posting information on a wiki that is inappropriate, inaccurate, or where postings may bully another student.
It is a good practice to develop the rules and guidelines for your wiki with your students and ensure that they have a positive tone. As in a traditional classroom, students are more likely to abide by rules that they have developed than ones imposed on them.

THE HORIZON PROJECT

The Horizon Project (http://horizonproject.wikispaces.com/) is an excellent example of how wikis can be used for collaborative education. It was selected as a 2007 finalist in the Edublog Awards for Best Educational Wiki. The Horizon Project is a collaborative global project between classrooms in diverse geographical locations. Students in grades 10-12 in The International School Dhaka, Bangladesh, Westwood Schools in Camilla, Georgia, Presbyterian Ladies College in Melbourne, Australia, the Vienna International School in Vienna, Austria and the Shanghai American School in Shanghai, China collaborated in this project. Through research and discussion on their wiki they envisioned the education and society of the future according to the six trends outlined in the Horizon Report 2007 Edition. (Horizon).

SUMMARY

Information literacy and communication is not a matter of knowing what source to use, but of being able to decide what source to use, based on the goal at hand. Confusion often arises as to when to use a wiki, a blog, or a discussion board forum.

A blog is used to communicate from one person to many people with the readers adding short comments to the blog. Several people working together with a final product as its goal usually choose to create a wiki. A discussion board forum encourages many users asking questions and letting many people answer. The emphasis of a discussion board is on conversation as compared to product building.

Using a wiki in a school and within a classroom improves communication and reinforces the constructionist style of learning. The wiki format cannot only be used for Wikipedia, but also a source for textbooks and student and teacher produced resources.

Chapter 10

Mashups

WHAT IS A MASHUP?

The term "mashup" originated from a musical composition
technique developed in the hip-hop world in which
musicians remixed tracts from other arts into a new piece of
music. Since that time, the combining of separate digital
content into a new and unique application has become
known as a mashup. (Ramos 1)

> **Mash-up** - refers to a new type of Web-based
> applications that mixes at least two different
> services from separate, and even competing, Web
> sites.

Carl Claunch, vice president and distinguished analyst at
Gartner, an information and technology research and
advisory firm headquartered in Stamford, Connecticut
suggested that by 2010, 80 percent of composite enterprise
applications will be built using Web mashups. (Lager) One
of the biggest social issues facing mashup developers is the
tradeoff between the protection of intellectual_property and
consumer privacy versus fair-use and the free flow of
information.

HOW MASHUPS WORK

To create a mashup users take APIs (Application Program
Interface) from multiple Web sites and merge them to form
new, innovative applications. In technology, a mashup is a

web application that combines data from more than one source into a single integrated tool.

> ***Application programming interface (APIs)*** - *a set of instructions that allow direct communication between software programs.*

EXAMPLES OF MASHUPS

One of the first mashups was the Hurricane Katrina Information Map created by Scipionus.com (http://www.scipionus.com/katrina.html). The people affected by Hurricane Katrina in 2005 who were trying to find information about the status of specific locations affected by the storm and its aftermath used this map to help make plans. (This site is no longer an active Web site.)

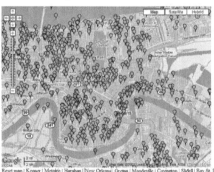

Figure 10:1 - Katrina

Since then, mashups are becoming commonplace in a multitude of different ways. The business community especially has found mashups a helpful marketing tool. For example, an employee at a chain of hardware stores can create a mashup that combines inventory data, storm forecasts, and the telephone numbers of branch managers.

When snow is forecast, the application sends text messages to the managers' cell phones, telling them how many shovels to order. (Eisenberg)

The real estate industry uses cartographic data from Google Maps to add location information to the real-estate data from Craigslist (see craigslist.org) creating a new and distinct web service that was not provided by either source. The description of a particular real estate contains a link to the Web site of the announcement. This site contains tags with the street and city name of the real estate. Housing maps then converts this address into its geographical coordinates and displays it on the map. The classic mashup is HousingMaps (http://www.housingmaps.com/) by Paul Rademacher, a 3-D graphic artist.

The photo-sharing site of Flickr links photos to locales by geotagging of their collection of photos at (http://flickr.com/map/) this enables users to organize photos by where they were taken, not just when. Stewart Butterfield, general manager and co-founder of Flickr has been quoted as saying, "Every photo was taken somewhere. That's almost always part of the story of the photo." In late 2007, Flickr houses 36 million geotagged photos--roughly 3 percent of its total archive. (Shankland)

Google Earth (http://earth.google.com/) combines the power of Google Search with satellite imagery, maps, terrain, and 3D buildings to put the world's geographic information at your fingertips. This Geographic Information System (GIS) allows users to move, zoom, tilt, and rotate the earth surface. A tremendous amount of usable information is available free of charge, Google Earth Pro has even more features for research and collaboration for $400.

CREATING YOUR OWN MASHUP

Google Maps is altering the way we find information on the web by creating a uniform way for people to find information on a map. Since June 2005, Google has been offering an API to their map service. This allows for an integration of maps into other Web pages and for customizations such as markers and overlays with data from other sources. According to the mashup/APItracking Web site Programmable Web, as of late 2006 some 45% of all mashups consisted of some manner of mapping application, and Google Maps was included in 51% of all mashups listed in their database. The majority of educational mashups are also based around Google Maps. (Mashups: Scottish Institute)

Teachers, students, and other users will have little difficulty finding innovative ways to incorporate geotagging into the curriculum or personal lives. Google developers can help educators create their own Google Maps mashup by contacting them at (http://www.gmapsdev.com/).

In 2007, a new feature in Google maps was added that would allow anyone to create their own map without needing to program or manipulate software other than embedding a few lines of HTML. You can drag and drop personalized place marks, routes, text descriptions, photos, or videos into a map. (http://maps.google.com/support/bin/answer.py?answer=68 480#overview)

The YouTube Data application program interface offers a simple and powerful way to access YouTube's content in the form of Google Data API feeds. You can create mashups of YouTube videos with other feeds or applications, such as news, photos, and maps by following the directions at http://code.google.com/apis/youtube/overview.html.

Another YouTube mashup is their remixer powered by Adobe Premier Express. This browser-based applet allows users to add captions, graphics, borders, and transitions to clips that have already uploaded to a person's YouTube account. You can try YouTube Remixer at (http://www.youtube.com/ytremixer/) and then publish your video clip on your own account of YouTube.

Yahoo's mash-up tool, Pipes (http://pipes.yahoo.com/pipes/docs?doc=overview) was

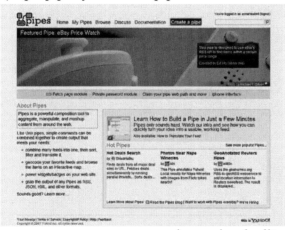

introduced in February 2007. It is a free online service that lets users remix popular feed types and create data mashups

Figure 10:2 – Yahoo! Pipes

using a visual editor. You can use Yahoo! Pipes to run your own web projects, or publish and share your own web services without ever having to write a line of code. No separate software plug-ins is required to use Pipes, since it features a drag and drop interface to help you build applications. Yahoo! Pipes permits for a great deal of customization and flexibility, but it also has a tough learning curve for the less experienced users.

Another new mash-up system, Popfly (http://www.popfly.com) from Microsoft, was released in a test form in April of 2007. Popfly's target audience is

Graphic 10:3 - Popfly

consumers, starting with the MySpace generation so they could embed their favorite mash-ups on their Web pages. Using Popfly users can enhance a social network where they can host, share, rate, comment, and even remix creations from other Popfly users. Pipes was developed for developers and Popfly was clearly designed for developers and users.

Popfly requires users to install extra software, called Silverlight that creates striking, three-dimensional representations of the data that users drag and drop in a central area of the screen and combine to create mash-ups.

The Popfly includes three tools:

1. Mashup Creator - lets users fit together pre-built blocks in order to mash together different web services and visualization tools.
2. Web Creator - a tool for creating Web pages.

3. Popfly Space - completed mashups and Web pages are stored in 25MB on Popfly Space, where users receive a customizable profile page and other social networking features.

Popfly lets user do much more than other mashup creators do yet it is one of the easiest to use web application interfaces. With Popfly, you can create applications, mashups, Web pages, and widgets (gadgets). These can be tied together in a social network (as part of the Live Spaces platform) where you can connect with other users and publishers of applications.

READY-MADE MASHUPS

If you want to take advantage of the mashup possibilities without creating one yourself, a good place to search for existing mashups is ProgrammableWeb (http://www.programmableweb.com), a clearinghouse of mashups, APIs, tools, and other mashup-related resources. It is a directory, a news source, a reference guide, a community.

To locate fifty things to do with Google Maps Mashups you can find suggestions at Google Maps Mania (http://googlemapsmania.blogspot.com/2007/12/50-more-things-to-do-with-google-maps.html).

MIXER TOOLS

Other mashup mixer tools to consider and explore for the wide possibilities for classroom, business, or personal use include:

1. Voice Threads (http://voicethread.com) - Records or imports video, audio, or add text to weave Flickr imported images into a media presentation.
2. VUVOX (http://www.vuvox.com/) - Turns photos, video, and music into professional quality presentations that can easily be shared.
3. FLEKTOR (http://www.flektor.com/) allows users to quickly and easily create, remix, and share photos, videos, with others via email, on MySpace, or in a blog.
4. Mixercast (http://www.mixercast.com/) allows users to mixing your images, video, and sound easily with unique templates and share across the web in one click.

APPLYING MASHUPS TO THE CURRICULUM

Google Lit Trips (http://www.googlelittrips.org/) harnesses Google Earth as a powerhouse-teaching tool for literature studies. The interactive Web-based application allows users to search the globe, using satellite imagery, maps, terrain, and other three-dimensional images. Google Earth enables teachers to make the information of a story more visible to students, and as a result, more discussable so that students achieve a deeper understanding of great literature.

A rich databases of real-time data, is Worldometers (http://www.worldometers.info/), which contains tickers continually updating data about world population, economics, education, environment, food, water, energy, and health. The immediate statistics can be applied not only to math assignments, but to social science problems as well.

The Gmaps Pedometer (http://www.gmap-pedometer.com/) can be used to map visually a walking route. This site updates the distance as more locations are added. Users can even add a calorie counter to the mashup. Students can use this mashup by estimating how far it is from home to school and then calculating the distance. With the addition of a calorie counter, they could figure how many calories they would burn if they walk to school instead of ride.

The Google Planimeter (http://www.acme.com/planimeter/) measures areas. This is done by clicking on three points on a map, and the Planimeter connects them in a triangle and computes the area. Clicking on additional points, the triangle expands into a many-sided polygon; the program will re-compute the area. Using this mashup, students can estimate the area of a geographical region; plot several points to obtain increasingly accurate estimates. If your class is studying a heavily populated area, they can combine this data with demographic data for further study.

Earthquakes in the Last Week (http://earthquakes.tafoni.net/) use Google Maps with data provided by the U.S. Geological Survey to show earthquakes of magnitude 2.5 or greater in the past seven days. Science teachers can use this mashup to study patterns, and then correlate them with plate tectonics and faults. Students can click the map markers for further information regarding the specific quake. (Branzburg)

SUMMARY

The use of mashups, the combining of totally unrelated APIs, application program interfaces, is quickly coming into common usage. Currently nearly half of all mashups integrates a factual database into Google maps, which helps users to better understand the world in which they live.

As the ease of preparing mashups improves, educators and students will discover a multitude of curriculum projects that can be enhanced with their use. Not only will teachers be preparing mashups, but students will be able to manipulate the data as well. This data manipulation will help develop students' reasoning and higher order thinking skills.

The use of mashups is becoming a vital tool for marketing within the business community and government officials have developed mashups for public safety and policy development. The possibilities of the mashup seem limitless.

Chapter 11

VIRTUAL OFFICE APPLICATIONS

WHAT ARE VIRTUAL OFFICES?

Virtual Offices provide cost-cutting methods to create, store, and collaborate information. By being able to access your work, or the work of others, in your workgroup or class, business people, educators, and students are able to work more efficiently and trace their productivity from any computer with an Internet connection. Several Web sites provide all, or limited services of a virtual office.

GOOGLE APPLICATIONS

The Web may not replace your traditional desktop applications if your needs go beyond basic e-mail, word processing, and spreadsheet tasks, or if your Internet connection is slow, but you may be surprised at how much you can do within a browser. However, there are activities that office suites let you do that you cannot do on locally installed applications. Virtual offices have the ability to collaborate on documents in real time, regardless of each person's physical location. They also provide online storage and auto-save, which means that you do not need to fear local hard drive failures or power outages.

In order to use Google applications a Google account must be established with an address and password of your choice. If you already have a Gmail account, Google applications are already available. Once you have a Google Account, you can go to the Google Docs homepage and sign in. The Google Account acts a secure authentication method to keep your online accounts private while also allowing you to access numerous Google services with a single sign-in. While it is possible to view a document, spreadsheet or presentation without a Google Account (via an invitation), you will need to create a Google Account to edit the document, spreadsheet or presentation, and to continue accessing Google Docs.

Google applications include Gmail, Google Talk, Google Calendar, Google Docs, Google Spreadsheets, Site, and iGoogle Start Page. The greatest advantage of using these applications is that they allow multiple users to access and modify the same document and provides them the chance to comment as they work together. Google hosts all these services; therefore, there is no hardware or software to install or download, and minimal setup and maintenance.

In October 2006, Google allowed educational institutions to sign-up for Google Apps for Education (http://www.google.com/educators/about.html) where they had assembled information, lesson plans, best practices, and tools. Google Apps Education Edition provides anywhere-anytime solutions that improve communication and collaboration among all members of the campus community.

GOOGLE DOCS

The strength of Google Docs is its ability to load Word documents, OpenOffice, RTF, HTML, text, or create documents from scratch. Users can easily do all the basic features, including making bulleted lists, sorting by columns, adding tables, images, comments, formulas, changing fonts, and more.

You can edit documents online wherever you are, then publish to the entire world, a select few, or keep your document private. You can also publish your documents online with one click, as normal-looking Web pages, without having to learn anything new. Once you have created a document, you can post it to your blog, and then select whomever you choose to have viewing and editing privileges and unpublish the document at any time.

To invite others to collaborate on your Google Docs you simply use the share tab by entering their email addresses. Here, you can add either individual email addresses, or the addresses of user groups. Anyone you have invited to either edit or view your document, spreadsheet, or presentation can access it as soon as he signs in. Multiple people can view and make changes at the same time. There is also an on-screen chat window for Google Docs and Spreadsheets users. Document revision history show you exactly who changed what, and when.

Selected users can view the revision history of your documents and spreadsheets and roll back to any version. With Google Docs, you can publish documents online to the world, as Web pages or post documents to your blog free of charge. Google Docs lets users share files and collaborate in real-time. Documents can be easily found by organizing them into as many folders as you want.

GOOGLE SPREADSHEET

Google Spreadsheet is able to import and export .xls, .csv, .txt, and .ods formatted data like any traditional spreadsheet. Users are able to format and edit formulas in spreadsheets as well as calculate results and make their data look the way they want. They can also chat in real time with others who are editing their spreadsheet as well as embed a spreadsheet, or a piece of a spreadsheet, in a blog or Web site.

GOOGLE PRESENTATIONS

Google Presentations is able to import existing presentations in .ppt and .pps file types as well as export presentations using the Save as Zip feature from the File menu. Users are able to insert images, and format slides to fit their preferences. Like Goggle Docs and Spreadsheet, users are able to share and edit each other's presentations in real-time from separate remote locations. They can also publish presentations on the web, allowing access to a wide audience by providing a URL that allows anyone, with or without a Google Account, to access and view the published document. Since Internet robots and spiders cannot access Google documents, spreadsheets or presentations, the published/shared URL must reference from pages outside of Google Docs to have it appear in Google's search index.

IGOOGLE START PAGE

The iGoogle Start Page is the first place your students will look to preview their inboxes and calendars, access their inbox, calendar, documents, campus information, and search the web from one place. On iGoogle users can combine their own content with additional external content and modules of their choice, and tailor the look and feel of the page with different logos, colors, and fonts.

GOOGLE COMMUNICATIONS

Gmail, Google Calendar, and Google Talk accounts help users to stay connected and work together more effectively. With Google Calendar, users are able to organize their schedule and share events with friends and coordinate schedules with friends and family -- all with one online calendar. With Google Calendar, you can see your friends' and family's schedules right next to your own; quickly add events mentioned in Gmail conversations or saved in other calendar applications; and add other interesting events that you find online. You can also set up automatic event reminders, including mobile phone notifications, and instantly bring up anything on your calendar with the built-in search tool.

GOOGLE NOTEBOOK

Google Notebook (www.google.com/notebook) is a free, interactive scratch pad for use on any visited Web pages. The Google Notebook allows you to collect information from the Internet and use it on any computer connected to the Internet. It leans toward the simple and sparse but provides a simple way to save and organize clips of information when conducting research online.

To use this feature you need to log in to your Google account and download the plug-in for Internet Explorer or Firefox. The next time you start your Internet browser, a notebook icon will appear in the lower right corner of the browser window. This personal browser tool permits you to write notes, and to clip text, images, and links from pages during browsing. These are saved to an online "notebook" with sharing and collaboration features. Sharing functions permits you to make public notebooks visible to others, or to collaborate with a list of other users (with or without making collaborative notebooks public).

Another feature of Google Notebooks allows you to keep all your notes organized by creating multiple notebooks for different subjects or by dividing a single notebook into several sections. You can also easily rearrange your notes by dragging-and-dropping them from one section or notebook to another.

Comments can be added to the clippings and you can use the search box at the top of the page to easily find any information in your notebooks. You can also invite your colleagues or students to collaborate on a notebook with you, giving them full access to edit that notebook and add their own notes. Those notebooks can be shared with everyone on the web by making it a public Web page as your published notebook will be assigned a unique web address that you can then share with friends and family.

You can organize your notes by adding section headings within a notebook by clicking the 'New note' button and then on the 'add section' link and you can rearrange your notes by dragging and dropping them from one section to another (or even from one notebook to another).
You can also export any notebook into Google Docs and Spreadsheets where you can edit your notebook as a document, collaborate with others, or publish it to the world.

SKETCHUP

Google SketchUp (http://sketchup.google.com/) is a powerful, yet easy-to-learn, 3D software tool that combines a simple, yet robust tool-set with an intelligent drawing system that streamlines and simplifies 3D design. If you use Google Earth, Google SketchUp allows you to place your models using real-world coordinates and share them with the world using the Google 3D Warehouse. (http://sketchup.google.com)

MICROSOFT OFFICE LIVE WORKSPACE

Microsoft Office Live Workspace (http://workspace.officelive.com/) is an online extension of Microsoft Office. It works with the programs you already know – Word, Excel, PowerPoint, and Outlook. You can open and save files directly from Microsoft Office XP, 2003, or 2007, as well as synchronize contact, tasks, and event lists with Outlook 2003 and 2007.

The workspace is an online place where you can save, access, and share documents and files. You can use it to group related information for work, school, or personal projects. Sharing is easy within this virtual office. All you need is a person's e-mail address and you can invite them to your workspace. The organizer has the power to decide if they can edit or simply review the workspace. You can access your workspace from any computer with an Internet connection and a Web browser.

ZOHO OFFICE SUITE

The Zoho Office Suite is a web office suite that includes tools for word processing, spreadsheets, presentations, databases, note taking, wikis, customer relations management, and other applications. The programs in the suite can be used individually but offer additional integration benefits when used together. Zoho Office Suite can also be used either to create content within its own programs or manipulate files created with other popular office suites such as Microsoft Office, OpenOffice, and other systems. Although some applications have Pro features available for a fee, Zoho has stated a commitment to maintain a free tier of entry-level applications. A single registration grants access to all the Zoho products.

Zoho has opened the Application Programming Interface (API) of its three major products: Zoho Writer, Zoho Sheet, and Zoho Show, which allows third parties to create programs that use the Zoho services. The Open Source API is able to synchronize with remote data from the web and allows users to build mashups with their software.

Zoho has created a plug-in to integrate their program into Microsoft Word and Excel, as well as a browser plug-in that can open text documents or spreadsheets without having word processing or spreadsheet applications installed on the local computer.

ZOHO WRITER

Zoho has recently released an online word processor that lets multiple users work on the document online and offline at the same time. When offline users go back online, the changes they made offline synchronizes with the online document. This is a useful feature for people who need to create and edit documents on planes and trains, or print from offices without wireless access. While an increasing number of applications allow this online-offline synchronizing, Zoho is one of a select few to offer a processor with this feature.

With the introduction of the iPhone, Zoho released a mobile version of Zoho Writer, Sheet, and Show called iZoho (http://mini.zoho.com/iZoho.jsp).

ZOHO SHEET

Zoho Sheet allows users to create and share interactive spreadsheets on the web. They can access their spreadsheets from anywhere, share documents with their friends and colleagues or publish them for public view, and allow multiple users to work on a spreadsheet simultaneously. Zoho Sheet allows users to copy-and-paste from Excel or imports an Excel file, as well as exports the file back to Excel.

ZOHO PLANNER

Zoho Planner is an online planner with a calendar, to-do lists, pages, and e-mail reminders that can be shared with different collaborators or groups. Zoho Planner competes with desktop features of Microsoft Outlook, and the online Google Calendar.

ZOHO MAIL

Zoho Mail is web-based collaboration groupware. It includes email, calendar, document management, task management, and contact management services.

ZOHO CHAT

Zoho Chat supports traditional private instant messaging. The script can be embedded into pages or blogs.

ZOHO SHOW

Zoho Show provides the ability to access, import, and edit presentations from anywhere. You can create slideshows directly in Zoho Show or import Microsoft PowerPoint (.ppt, .pps) or OpenOffice Presentation (.odp, .sxi) files. The slideshows created can be embedded in your blog or Web site.

ZOHO CREATOR

Zoho Creator is an online database/custom application development tool that allows users to create sophisticated process logic without knowing how to code, simply by dragging and dropping script elements on screen. You can import data from .xls, .csv, and .tsv files and create a variety of forms either from scratch or by using one of several common templates.

ZOHO MEETING

Zoho Meeting is an online meeting service to show/share users desktop online, conduct Web meetings, or troubleshoot/provide remote assistance to colleagues, students, or customers. All that is needed is a browser and an Internet connection for conducting a meeting. With Zoho Meeting, users can host live Web conferences and chat with all participants. Participants can edit, and share meeting online and join from anywhere with whomever they choose. The meeting can be saved and embedded inside Zoho Show, Zoho Notebook or any public Web page or blog.

ZOHO PROJECTS

Zoho's Project management software supports creating tasks, assigning ownership, setting deadlines, and tracking milestones. With this software, users can work with calendars, Gantt charts, reports, and share supporting files.

Zoho Projects is free for one project, and has a scaled price structure after that.

ZOHO WIKI

Zoho Wiki is as easy to use as a word processor. Users can create groups to develop a wiki and then, add, edit, and share contents among their group. Participants can have multiple versions of content pages, and not merely multiple copies, as well as the ability organize a site with subpages for each page. All public wiki pages are indexed and cached by search engine robots and hence will be listed in search results of multiple search engines.

ZOHO NOTEBOOK

Zoho Notebook allows you to create different types of content from text, image, audio, video, etc, and aggregate your information in one place. Users can embed content of any type from multiple applications as well as share an entire book, page, or just an object on a page by granting read/write permissions. This software allows users to keep track of changes not only at the book or page level but also at the object level.

ZOHO CHALLENGE

Zoho Challenge is an online test and evaluation application for users that is free for up to 25 participants. This software supports both multiple choice and descriptive questions and the results are displayed immediately. You can add students; schedule test months in advance, view a report card, and view graphical representation of the overall results of tests.

THINKFREE OFFICE SUITE

ThinkFree (http://thinkfree.com/) is a Microsoft Office compatible application suite containing word processing, spreadsheet, and presentation graphics software that are usable both online and off. ThinkFree Office features Internet-based file sharing and 1GB of online storage, as well as end-to-end security. ThinkFree Office is compatible with Windows, Macintosh, UNIX, and Linux systems.

OPENOFFICE.ORG

OpenOffice.org (http://www.openoffice.org/) is an office suite application available for several computer operating systems. OpenOffice.org is a collection of applications that work together closely to provide the features expected from a modern office suite. They aim to compete with Microsoft Office and copy its look and feel whenever possible. OpenOffice can read and write most of the file formats found in Microsoft Office as well as many other applications.

Components of OpenOffice include:

1. Writer - A word processor similar to Microsoft Word that offers a comparable range of functions and tools.
2. Calc - A spreadsheet similar to Microsoft Excel.
3. Base - A database program similar to Microsoft Access.
4. Draw - A vector graphics editor comparable in features to CorelDRAW. It has similar features to Desktop publishing software such Microsoft Publisher.
5. Impress - A presentation program similar to Microsoft PowerPoint.

6.   Math - A tool for creating and editing mathematical formulae, similar to Microsoft Equation Editor.

7.   The macro recorder - Used to record user actions and replay them later to help with automating tasks.

8.   QuickStarter - A small program for Windows and Linux that runs when the computer starts for the first time.

OpenOffice is free of charge, but it does not meet the criteria of a virtual office since it resides on a local desktop and not a server over the Internet. You will need to download all the OpenOffice features together, but not all of them will need to be installed on the hard drive. Collaboration does not occur in the use of the product, but in the development and improvement of the software.

OpenOffice.org is an Open Source project. This means, that that they offer not only a product for end-users, but it is also a process. OpenOffice depends upon the contributions of developers and end-users to make that process happen. Once users have registered, they are entitled to join particular projects, file issues, bugs, patches, or comment on already filed issues.

USES OF VIRTUAL OFFICE WITHIN THE CURRICULUM

Each tool in a virtual office offers a specific set of features. One primary use of virtual office software within the curriculum is for collaboration using Documents and Spreadsheets. These tools can help teachers track collaboration, revisions, and teamwork through RSS feeds. By tracking the revisions, teachers are able to see if students are on task and can identify the written portion of contributions by group members to the project or assignment.

Teaching collaborative revision is a critical piece of the writing process and helps to fulfill the stated goal of The National Council of Teachers of English, which espouses writing as a process and encourages multiple revisions and peer editing. Google Docs has collaborated with Weekly Reader's Writing for Teens magazine (http://www.google.com/educators/weeklyreader.html) to help you teach collaboration in a meaningful and practical way.

Some of the ways classroom teachers may choose to use the word processing tool included in virtual office software include:

- Co-editing essays
- Collaborative research papers
- Creative writing
- Collaborative book reports
- Writing materials for student portfolios

Ways in which the spreadsheet tool included with a virtual office package can be incorporated into the curriculum includes:

- Teachers keeping track of student progress
- Teachers maintaining group work information
- Teachers maintaining mailing lists
- Students keeping track of class assignments
- Students or teachers planning and tracking expenses on a trip, for a party, or weekly expenses
- Students planning for college expenses

Online presentation software offers alternatives for students who do not have presentation or slideshow software at home. They can create and collaborate with their peers online and then use the Web site to make their presentations. Some of these tools offer tagging and commenting on any presentation, which makes finding similar presentations easier.

ONLINE PDF CONVERTERS

Information obtained on a Web site can be archived more easily and shared in PDF format than any other format. Whenever a formatted document needs to retain its formatting while being transferred electronically often a PDF format is the best, particularly if the receiver does not have the same program.

To convert the major Microsoft format documents on a desktop computer to PDF format an online PDF converter is a fast, easy tool to use. After uploading a file, within minutes the PDF document will arrive in the sender's e-mail box. Users can access a free online URL to PDF Converter at http://www.html-to-pdf.net/free-online-pdf-converter.aspx or use PDF Online (http://www.pdfonline.com/) from BCL Technology among other sites.

ONLINE SURVEY TAKER

Educators, business people, and government workers often have need for a quick, easy method to survey others. SurveyMonkey (http://www.surveymonkey.com/) has proved to be a safe, simple way to create online surveys and analyze the results.

ONLINE PERSONAL FILE STORAGE

When students, teachers, and business people need to share large files without posting them on a public site a personal file storage service may meet their needs. Online storage space in designed for individuals, in need of *network storage* for personal backup, file access, or file distribution. Users can upload their files, access them from anywhere with Internet connections, and share the password only with those desired.

Most online file storage services offer space on a per-gigabyte basis — some charge for the service while others offer the service free of charge since they rely on advertising revenue. Some services require a software download, which makes files only available on computers on which that software is installed while other services allow users to retrieve files through any web browser. With the increased inbox space offered by webmail services, many users have started using their webmail service as an online drive. Some sites offer free unlimited file storage but have a limit on the file size.

ONLINE FAX SERVICE

Internet Fax (also known as e fax, email fax, online fax, and digital fax) utilizes an Internet fax service provider to convert a facsimile transmission into a digital file that can be sent and received via email. Internet fax services bridge the gap between the older fax technology, and the email transmission of documents.

When users sign up with an Internet fax service, they will be assigned a dedicated fax phone number that will convert incoming faxes to email attachments that are automatically sent to their email address. The majority of these services allow users to send attachments (like Word documents, PDF's, or pictures) to physical fax numbers that are received just as if they were sent from a standard fax machine. Most Internet fax services will send documents in a number of different file formats, such as TIF or PDF files.

Popular Internet fax services include eFAX (http://home.efax.com) and Myfax (www.myfax.com). Features to consider in selecting an Internet Fax Services is found at http://www.faxcompare.com/.

JOTT

Jott (http://jott.com/) lets users communicate with their local computer or favorite computer sites on the go by sending voice e-mails and text messages. Jott Apps helps users stay organized the way that works best for them, whether they want the simplicity of a desktop list application in Jott Express, are obsessed with their BlackBerry, or they need immediate access to Outlook or iGoogle HomePage.

Jott Links let users post to many web services with merely their voice. Among other things, users can check prices on Amazon.com, add an appointment to a Google Calendar, or update your followers on Twitter, with a simple phone call to Jott.

SUMMARY

Educators and business people are quickly discovering the effectiveness of using a Virtual Office Application not only to collaborate with peers, but also to help others share information and work together as a team. The availability of accessing their work from any computer connected to the Internet greatly enhances time management possibilities for Virtual Office users.

The format of Virtual Office Application may vary from one to another. Some software applications allow users to download the software onto the desktop or laptop computer and then upload their work when desired while other programs allow users to work directly on their private or public virtual office space. The creators of some software maintain strict control over their applications, while others are Open Source, where anyone with sufficient knowledge can make changes to the coding of the program itself.

Chapter 12

VIRTUAL LEARNING ENVIRONMENTS (VLE)

DEVELOPING E-LEARNING COURSES

E-learning provides learning resources in electronic media and makes them available 'anywhere, anytime.' Occasionally the required production skills can be beyond teachers' experience, and it is tempting to have the course publication done by commercial publishers, or a specialist, or web unit. This can have the effect of de-professionalizing the teachers, who lose control of the materials they want to use with their students.

Even where teachers do remain in control of learning materials, a common mistake is simply to publish resources appropriate to the course. Such content may be interactive but if the students passively consume the information it can alienate students who feel reduced to the level of recipients of content rather than participants in learning. Creating courses with forums, peer-assessed workshops, journals, surveys, and interactive lessons is more work than creating a course from a series of static Web pages.

The most important part of developing an e-learning course is to have a clear understanding of the educational standards, goals, and objectives desired. Everything done to prepare for the course should be done with those objectives in mind.

The next major step in developing an e-learning course is the selection of the authoring tools. In order to save time and money, these tools need to be easy to use and allow for the automation of as much multimedia production as possible. When selecting the authoring tools, consideration of the type of course desired should be a top priority.

COURSE MANAGEMENT PROGRAMS

There are two basic types of e-learning courses: information-based and performance-based. Knowing the difference will help you design the best course appropriate to your standards, objectives, and goals. Many online courses are not technically e-learning courses, but e-information ones. The goal of these courses is not to change performance as much as it is to share new information. How you approach this type of course is different from how you design a performance-based course. (Kuhlmann 21)

In designing a performance-based course, you will want to build it so the course mimics real life as much as possible. You want the students to make real-world decisions with observable consequences that extend beyond the computer, which allow you to provide valuable feedback based on the decisions the learner makes. (Kuhlmann 29)

An entry point for blog use at the school level can be to build a class portal to communicate information about the class and to archive course materials. From a teaching standpoint, having a place to publish the course curriculum, syllabus, class rules, homework assignments, rubrics, handouts, and presentations makes a blog a powerful course management tool. Coupled with a classroom portal space, there is a possibility that a class can go paperless as students simply post their work online for peer and teacher responses. This creates a digital filing cabinet for students to archive their work and, in effect, creates a space for an online portfolio of their work.

A basic Wiki as discussed in chapter nine can be designed as a course management system, but it will lack the additional features of a virtual learning environment. Wikis are generally used as only one component of a complex course system. The distinguishing characteristic of a course management program (CMS) is that they are Web sites that are built and updated by supplying information in a web format. CMSs involve template Web pages that include the visual elements that will appear on every page in the site. This can include the banner, footer, school or institution name, and main menu.

Teachers wanting to teach online can use learnhub (http://learnhub.com/), which provides them with their own online learning portal. Teachers can add courses that anyone can find and enroll in as well as charge for the online courses. They can manage students, class curriculum, quizzes, and more importantly, learn pages (allowing for headings, text, files, images, and video) that their students will be reading throughout the class.

Sakai (http://www.sakaiproject.org/portal /) is an online Collaboration and Learning Environment. Many users of Sakai deploy it to support teaching and learning, collaboration, as well as support for portfolios.

A robust commercial online course management system that is common at the university level is the Blackboard Learning System (http://www.blackboard.com/). It offers an open architecture for customization and interoperability, and a scalable design that allows for integration with student information systems and authentication protocols.

Another commercial online course management system is Desire2Learn (http://www.desire2learn.com/), which assists in the delivery of online learning for Schools, Colleges, Universities, and Corporations.

MOODLE

Although some schools invest in expensive content management systems such as Blackboard (http://www.blackboard.com) or Desire2Learn (http://www.desire2learn.com) many free online blog and content management systems packages such as Moodle (http://www.moodle.com) and Engrade (http://www.engrade.com/) can accomplish almost as much at little or no cost.

Moodle is a free, Open Source course management system (CMS) designed to help educators create effective online learning communities and is currently the most popular distance learning content management system (CMS) in K-12 education. Moodle was created by Martin Dougiamas, a WebCT (a course management system now owned by BlackBoard) administrator at Curtin University, Australia. Moodle has been evolving since 1999 and has been using the current architecture since 2001.

The word Moodle was originally an acronym for **M**odular **O**bject-**O**riented **D**ynamic **L**earning **E**nvironment. Moodle is also a verb that describes the process of lazily meandering through something, doing things as it occurs to you to do them, an enjoyable tinkering that often leads to insight and creativity. As such, it applies both to the way Moodle was developed, and to the way a student or teacher might approach studying or teaching an online course. Anyone who uses Moodle is a Moodler.

The popular course management system is designed to support an interactive learning style called *Social*

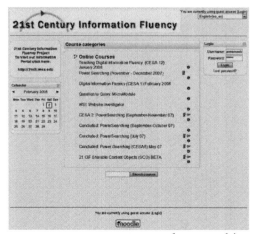

Constructionist Pedagogy. The social constructionist philosophy believes that people learn best when they interact with the learning material, construct new material for others, and interact with other students about the material. The difference between a traditional class and the social constructionist philosophy is the difference between a lecture and a discussion. (Rice, 9)

Graphic 12:1 Moodle

Teachers can use Moodle to organize learning content as a course divided into modules and lessons complete with discussions, quizzes, and tests. Users can often integrate these modules into the school or district student-information system. Moodle has features that promote collaboration, activities, reflection, and other characteristics for both online classes and face-to-face learning. Moodle keeps detailed logs of all activities that users perform on a site. These logs can be used to determine who has been active in a particular site, what they did, and when they did it.

Users can also upload any type of file into Moodle. The user's web browser accesses the files through Moodle, so it is important to use only formats that are commonly used on the web for images, MP3 files, Flash files, and Adobe Acrobat documents. Embedded Flash files are used for all video since most computers have the Flash player and users do not have to install downloads and players.

The social format of instruction is very different from a traditional sequential course. The social format of Moodle turns the entire course into a discussion forum, and offers users the chance to put a discussion forum right into the course listings. Discussion topics are displayed on the course's home page. Students can reply to a topic they are reading by clicking on "Discuss this topic."

The Moodle Wiki module enables students to collaborate on a book-like writing project. Because a Wiki is easy to use, interactive, and organized by date, it encourages informal discussion among the participants. The course creator is able to determine who can edit the Wiki and who can see it.

The workshop activity is the most complex tool currently available in Moodle. A workshop provides a place for the students in a class to see a sample project, upload their individual projects, see and assess other student's projects. When a teacher requires each student to assess the work of several other students, the workshop becomes a powerful collaborative grading tool. Workshops can be ungraded, peer graded, instructor graded, or a combination of peer and instructor graded. Workshops enable users to create very specific assessment criteria for the graders to use along with setting due dates for submitting and grading work.

Users can download Moodle on any compatible computer. It is flexible enough to scale from a single-teacher site to a University with 200,000 students. Moodle is also available in a variety of download packages (http://download.moodle.org/) with different levels of stability, as well as via CVS (Concurrent Versions System). When installed on a local server Moodle only takes 60 MB of disk space. A number of additional modules/plugins (http://moodle.org/mod/data/view.php?id=6009) and language packs (http://download.moodle.org/lang16/) are also available.

Another option if a local server is not available is ClassroomRevolution.com (http://www.classroomrevolution.com/ who has partnered with Moodle to provide Moodle Hosting Services. All of their hosting accounts are installed on dedicated, Moodle-optimized servers in Dallas, Texas. Each of these dedicated and shared servers is expertly configured and provides many value-added services.

In Moodle 1.8.2, an activity drop-down menu was added containing a number of robust interactive learning activity modules that can be added to a course. Communication and collaboration may take place using live real-time Chats or asynchronous discussion forums for conversational activities. Users can also use Choices to gain group feedback. Online Quizzes offer several options for automatic and manual scoring. Survey and Choice give teachers the opportunity to assess students, their attitudes toward learning, and their satisfaction with a course. Glossaries of keywords can be set up by the instructor, and can be configured to allow students to edit, add, or rate entries.

PREPARING MEDIA FOR A COURSE MANAGEMENT SYSTEM

Providing clear audio is essential if multimedia will be provided with the e-course. There are multitudes of resources and Web sites available that will assist e-course developers as well as online communities for the specific software used. Many of the suggestions in chapter seven of this book pertaining to preparing audio for podcasting also applies to preparing audio for an e-course.

Video consumes a great deal of bandwidth and is a drain on a school's network unless it is an embedded link. Before you commit to using video in your e-course, you may need to check that your school has the infrastructure and technology available for the end users.

When preparing video for an e-course, it is important to remember that 'shorter is better.' To avoid losing viewers, make it a habit never to exceed three to four minutes on a single video. If you make screencasting videos such as software demos, it is important to keep them as short as possible to save file size. Audio explanations need to be direct and beneficial so the viewer is not spending time watching the mouse fly back and forth.

ONLINE GRADE BOOKS AND OTHER TOOLS

Several sites are available that are not full course management systems, but provide additional modules for established management systems or can stand alone as tools for traditional resource retrieval, assessment, and communication methods.

Engrade (http://www.engrade.com/) is a free online grade book that allows teachers to manage their classes online as well as post grades, assignments, attendance, and upcoming homework online for students and parents to see. Engrade automatically calculates grades, and provides custom grading scales, weighted assignments. It also provides easy attendance records, and automatically emails parents of absentees. Teachers can posts upcoming homework for parents and students to access in real-time.

Chalksite (http://www.chalksite.com/) is a web package designed just for teachers by providing a personal Web site and user-friendly tools to help manage their classes. Chalksite is designed for teachers, students, and parents to have a central point to access grading, assignments, discussions, and messaging.

ONLINE RUBRIC BUILDERS

Assessment is often one of the most difficult challenges educators face. Many teachers have found that rubrics enable an evaluation of student performance in situations that more closely replicate the challenges of real life than isolated tests. A rubric is a device for organizing and interpreting data gathered from observations of student performance.

> **Rubric** - a scoring guide that differentiates between levels of development in a specific area of performance or behavior.

Rubrics differ from traditional methods of assessment in that they examine students in the actual process of learning by showing them how their work is being evaluated. Rubrics provide detailed explanations of what is expected throughout a project and provide a clear teaching directive. The downside of grading using a rubric is that the preparation of rubrics for individual projects can be extremely time consuming. However, a large number of online rubric generators are available free of charge. Teachers merely select the categories and criteria for excellence expected for each category and the program prepares a rubric in an organized, easy to understand format. An extensive guide to using rubrics for assessment is found at http://school.discoveryeducation.com/schrockguide/assess.html.

The following sites each have special features and some are more complicated to use than others are.

- Rubistar (http://rubistar.4teachers.org/index.php)
- Rubric Machine (http://landmark-project.com/rubric_builder/index.php)
- Teach4Learning Rubric Maker (http://myt41.com/) -- Click on Tools and then Rubric Maker.
- TeAchnology (http://www.teach-nology.com/web_tools/rubrics/) contains a collection of additional sites that have rubric construction online or software.

LEARNING AND RESEARCH RESOURCES

While some of these services technically may not be categorized as a Web 2.0 program, they are welcomed tools to assist with virtual learning.

MATHMATIC TOOLS

Create a Graph (http://nces.ed.gov/nceskids/createagraph/) is a free tool from The National Center for Education Statistics (NCES), located within the U.S. Department of Education that aims to make it easy for students to create bar graphs, line graphs, area graphs, pie charts, and point graphs.

Calcoolate (http://www.calcoolate.com/) provides users with a simple calculator with advanced expression support, mathematic functions, and history for viewing past calculations.

e-Tutor Graphing Calculator (http://www.e-tutor.com/et2/graphing/) is an advanced web-based graphing calculator that allows students to enter one or more equations and view them with position/intersection indicators and zooming functionality.

BIBLIOGRAPHY GENERATORS

All fields of research agree on the need to document intellectual borrowing, but documentation formats vary among the different scholarly disciplines. Broadly speaking the MLA (Modern Language Association) (http://www.mla.org/style) style guide is with the humanities and the APA (American Psychological Association) (http://www.apastyle.org/) style guide is use with the sciences. To simplify the layout and punctuation in preparing a bibliography or works cited several bibliography generators are available online. With these programs users merely enter the appropriate data and the program arranges it in the correct format. The most popular programs include Noodletools.com (http://www.noodletools.com/), Citation Maker, (http://citationmachine.net/) and EasyBib (http://www.easybib.com/).

TIMELINE GENERATORS

Interactive timelines are designed to allow users to easily display relationships between items. These timelines can serve as a productivity tool by displaying project planning and deadlines along with helping users summarize a sequence of events or organize their understanding of content specific information.

Popular timeline generators include:

1. Read/Write/Think Timeline Generator (http://www.readwritethink.org/materials/timeline/) - an interactive tool that invites users to generate descriptive timelines that can be plotted with their choice of units of measure.

2. Dandelife (http://dandelife.com) generates a timeline of any kind of event in a person's life. Users can write as blog-like entry, apply tags, and attach images, videos, bookmarks from other Web sites.

3. OurStory (http://www.ourstory.com/) allows users to write a 'story' about what happened on a date in time, add pictures, video, and the program will create a timeline.

4. xtimeline (http://xtimeline.com/) - a powerful and well-designed timeline in which images can be attached and media embed.

PROJECT MANAGEMENT FOR CHILDREN

Thinkquest (http://www.thinkquest.org/) is an online learning community run by Oracle's Education Foundation. This software helps students become multimedia authors who use Web sites and interactive tools to collaborate on projects, build knowledge together, and publish their ideas.

MasteryMaze (www.masterymaze.com) is a learning community site designed to provide a safe space for collaboration among teachers, as well as a space for students to share, discuss, and achieve MASTERY in the classroom. The Maze, like the classroom, will contain review podcasts and videos created by teachers around the world. It is designed to assist teaching and learning curricular subjects such as history, math, science, and more.

CARTOON STRIP GENERATORS

Teachers and parents often use comic strip games to encourage students to improve language, reading, storytelling and creative skills. Two popular cartoon strip generators for children include Thinkquest and MakeBeliefComix. Many other cartoon strip generators for all age levels can be found by using any search engine.

Creating a cartoon strip using the online tool from the Read Write Think organization (http://www.readwritethink.org/materials/comic/) is an excellent launching point for students with limited computer skills. The interface is easy to navigate and the student can choose from a variety of objects to add to their cartoon along with background and caption bubbles. MakeBeliefComix (http://www.makebeliefscomix.com) is also an easy way to use comic strip generator for use with children where they can create their own comics and print them out or email them.

SUMMARY

Participating in a virtual learning environment is not only becoming popular at the University level, but is becoming widely used in the K-12 and business environments as well. The most important part of developing an e-learning course is to have a clear understanding of the educational standards, goals, and objectives desired. Online learning resources come in a multitude of electronic media formats that are made available anywhere, anytime. Much of the online content may be interactive which is able to engage students and lead to deeper understanding. Creating courses with forums, peer-assessed workshops, journals, surveys, and interactive lessons is more work than creating a course from a series of static Web pages.

Chapter 13

SOCIAL NETWORKING

WHAT IS SOCIAL NETWORKING?

In the traditional sense, social networking is the process of initiating, developing, and maintaining friendships and collegial or professional relationships for mutual benefit. However, the current usage of social networking generally refers to activities utilizing web-based tools for interaction and collaboration. Social networks bring another dimension to the Web beyond simple links between Web pages, by adding links between people and communities.

Social networks are not just a collection of people seeking long lost friends, teens creating mischief online, or sexual predators lurking behind a keyboard; Social networks create a new and unique opportunity to share not only written ideas, but visual and musical creations as well, with everyone unbound by the physical limits created by the location where one lives. (Draggon 34)

Some of the first social networking Web sites such as Classmate.com and Friendster.com were places where you could find old high school friends or build up a list of friends from around the world. Soon after its founding in 2003, the Web site MySpace.com has become one of the largest social networking sites in the world. Older teens, young adults, and adults are attracted to Facebook.com for both personal and professional use. Most recent politicians and activists make use of Facebook to spread their message and connect to a wider audience.

Since the terminology of social networking is overburdened with negative connotations, when these tools are used within an educational environment, it would be better to refer to the activities involved as "professional networking" and "student networking" instead. Much of the technology-facilitated educational networking is done in the form of person-to-person exchanges that can be classified as question and answer or comment and response. The technologies that facilitate social networking tend to emphasize ease of use, spontaneity, and personalization.

HOW DO SOCIAL NETWORKS WORK?

The structure of social networks varies but most follow the following formula. Once a user signs up to be a member they will have their own page where they can usually add a photo and information about themselves or their hobbies. A user can search for other people who share the same interests, add them to a friend's list, or others can add that person to their friend's list. Friends can post messages to each other's pages and communicate in live chat or in chat rooms. (Draggon 34)

The layout of a social network usually contains:

- Authentication when joining
- The Home page
- A Side bar
- Subset Networks (members, groups, friends)
- User's Personal Page
- Media sharing displays

STUDENT AND EDUCATOR SOCIAL NETWORKING DIFFERENCES

Each person and profession brings their own background, style, and interest into an online social network, the same as they do to a face-to-face network. In helping students broaden their use of social networking, these differences are apparent:

- Professional educators use social networking more deliberately while students use it more naturally.
- Educators usually use it in just one dimension—for example, professionally but not personally, or vice versa, while students tend to use social networking in all phases of their lives.
- Professional educators use social networking to improve their teaching, plus make and keep in touch with friends and colleagues.
- Educators use it to understand ways of being near the way students learn. Educators create theories about its use and analyze its advantages and disadvantages in the classroom.
- Some Educators are hesitant or resistant to allow it to encompass their personal life and prefer to maintain more privacy.
- Students view social networking as a part of how they communicate and do not think of it any differently than using a cell phone.
- Students are social with social networks and use them for making plans, keeping up with schoolwork, chatting, sharing pictures, and videos.
- Students have faster thumbs. They use SMS (short message service) as a social network, while most adults without Blackberries find that too tedious.

- Students frequently socialize and work simultaneously while to adults the social and work aspects are mutually exclusive. (Social)

SOCIAL NETWORKING SITES

GOOGLE'S OPENSOCIAL NETWORKING

The web can be more interesting when you can build applications that easily interact with your friends and colleagues. With the trend toward more social applications comes a growing number of site-specific APIs (**application program interface**) that users must learn. However, with Web sites sharing common APIs, it means you have less to learn to build on multiple Web sites.

Google is currently developing OpenSocial (http://code.google.com/apis/opensocial/) in conjunction with members of the web community. OpenSocial is built upon Google Gadget technology, so users can build a social application with little to no serving costs and without a server. Of course, users can also host their application on their own servers if they prefer. The ultimate goal is for any social Web site to be able to implement the APIs and host third party social applications.

OpenSocial is simple and straightforward yet also capable of developing full-blown, rich Internet applications without server-side infrastructure. It is based on open source standards with only minor proprietary lock-ins. Its documentation and sample code all use the Creative Commons licensing. Models like OpenSocial and its open source social platforms are ushering in a new era in competency in social software.

WINDOWS LIVE

The Windows Live service (www.live.com) offers PC users a social networking site where they can set up a profile and add friends. This service provides the option of downloading all the services with a single Unified Installer program, or as separate components. The individual services include Windows Live Photo Gallery, Windows Live Mail, Windows Live Messenger 8.5 and the security program Windows Live OneCare Family Safety. This software also includes the Windows Live Writer blogging application, while it carefully avoids cannibalizing two of Microsoft's mainstays, the Word and Excel programs.

SkyDrive online data storage service and its FolderShare service recently have been incorporated into Windows Live. SkyDrive currently gives test users one gigabyte of free Internet storage, while FolderShare makes it possible to synchronize between multiple computers — including Apple's Macintosh computers.

Microsoft designed Windows Live as a safe Web site management system by filtering the Web sites they visit. Built-in contact approval parents know whom their children are talking to on IM, e-mail, or their blogs and you can approve or reject each new contact for their Windows Live Messenger, Hotmail and Spaces. They provide age-specific default settings based on the recommendations of the American Academy of Pediatrics and other trusted sources. These settings can be adjusted to fit the needs and values of individual children.

SOCIAL NETWORKING FOR PROFESSIONAL AND CAREER DEVELOPMENT

It is a misnomer to use the term social network for sites used for education, collaboration, communication, business, or professional development. A more descriptive term would be student, teacher, administrator, business, or professional networking. Educational networking sites combine many of the tools of Web 2.0 into a structured environment: forum discussions, blogging, chat, messaging, email, and video-, photo-, and file- sharing. By bringing users together in an inclusive environment, social networks make it much easier for users to connect with each other and with discussions that are of interest. Online social networking provides a forum in which the informal learning can take place without being limited to time and place.

LINKEDIN

LinkedIn (http://www.linkedin.com/) is an online network of more than 30 million experienced professionals from around the world, representing 150 industries. When users join the network, they can create a profile that summarizes their professional accomplishments. Their profile helps users find and be found by former colleagues, clients, and partners. They can add more connections by inviting trusted contacts to join LinkedIn and connect to them. A person's LinkedIn network consists of their connections, their connections' connections, and the people they know, linking a user to thousands of qualified professionals.

Through the LinkedIn network users can:

- Get introduced to other professionals through the people they know
- Discover inside connections that can help them find employment
- Post and distribute job listings
- Search for jobs
- Be located for business or career opportunities
- Find potential clients, service providers, subject experts, and partners who come recommended

NING

While many social networks have networks that users join based on their interests, Ning (http://www.ning.com/) is a unique social networking Web site that allows users to create their own professional network. Ning has all of the features that other social networks offer while filtering out members and content that are not appropriate for school. Setting up a Ning is an easy way to set up a page that contains video, pictures, and a blog without knowing any programming.

To create a network on Ning, users will first name their network and determine if it will be public or private. Public networks can be joined by anyone while private networks are by invitation only. Choosing a private or public setting when you create a Ning Web site is a permanent choice. A private network that requires an invitation that cannot be changed to a public Web site anyone can join later. In a classroom setting, creating a private network is probably the best option. This insures that only users who are approved by the site organizer can join the network. The content of the Web site will be hidden from non-members when the "private" option is selected.

After the site organizer describes his Ning network, he can then choose the features he wants to include. To add features to a network, simply select options from the left side of the screen and drag them onto the layout template in the center of the screen. Ning will automatically do all the programming needed to set up forums, blog, music, or video sections of the Web site.

Once a person has completed the setup phase, he can launch his new education network by typing in the URL (http://your_social_network_name.ning.com).

Examples of Education Social Networking Sites Include:

- Classroom 2.0 (www.classroom20.com) is a social network for educators who are interested in the use of Web 2.0 and other collaborative technologies in the classroom. It was designed to help educators, especially those who did not have any experience with Web 2.0, to quickly feel comfortable participating.
- EduBloggerWorld (http://edubloggerworld.ning.com/) was created to facilitate connections and community among educational bloggers worldwide. Participants in the EduBloggerWorld community do not need to be technology gurus but merely need a desire to improve teaching and learning and a desire to improve community among educators worldwide.
- Ning in Education (http://education.ning.com/) is a community

of educators using Ning to build social networks.

NEXO

Nexo (http://www.nexo.com/) was created to simplify management of friends and family, work and sports teams, and community involvement. It was recently acquired by the photo-sharing site Shutterfly. Group management is built-in and customizable, and your group permissions can be set to ensure appropriate security for your group.

Nexo lets users easily create group Web sites, with shared calendars, forums, pictures, videos, etc. It lets users blog as a group, and integrates with other Web sites and e-mail. Group members are notified automatically when new information is added. Group widgets such as polls, roster updates, invites, and forums take the mess out of group decision making and feedback.

TAPPED IN

Tapped In (http://tappedin.org) is an educational professional development community that is owned and operated by SRI International Center for Technology in Learning (ctl.sri.com). It went online in 1997, with funding by a national Science Foundation grant. Tapped In brings educators together, both locally and worldwide, in order to cultivate a community that supports each individual teacher as a professional. At this site, educators at all levels come together to learn, collaborate, share, and support one another. This network focuses on significant issues in learning and teaching, and on the ways that innovative uses of technologies can help address those issues.

Tapped In provides multiple means of synchronous (real-time) and asynchronous (delayed) communication between members. These include chat, private messaging, discussion boards, and e-mail. The primary and most immediate of these is chat.

APPLE LEARNING INTERCHANGE (ALI)

The Apple Learning Interchange (ALI) (http://edcommunity.apple.com/ali/) is a social network for educators primarily using the Apple platform. A wealth of content ranging from simple lesson ideas to in-depth curriculum units for K-12 educators is available on this site as well as a new channel for Higher Education faculty displaying campus projects, research, and more. The Learning Interchange now provides a range of tools to support online collaboration in public and private groups.

SOCIAL/EDUCATIONAL NETWORKS IN THE CLASSROOM

TAKINGITGLOBAL

TakingITGlobal (http://www.takingitglobal.org/) is one of the best examples of how students are using digital technologies to transform the world around them. With 110,000 registered members in nearly two hundred countries, a Web site in seven languages, and five million unique visitors. TakingITGlobal consists of a set of tools and curricular activities that will help students collaborate with students in other countries in order to complete interactive learning projects that make a difference in their communities.

Cofounder Jennifer Corriero calls TakingITGlobal "a platform to support collaboration among young people in developing projects, in understanding and grappling with issues, and influencing the decision-making processes, especially around those issues that are directly affecting young people." (Tapscott 50- 51)

TakingITGlobal.org increases student engagement through applying social networking and user-created content principles. Already, thousands of teachers from dozens of countries have harnessed the power of user-created web content as the basis for informal assignments and experiential learning through the TakingITGlobal Initiative. Informal content creation gives students who might not be confident in their writing skills an opportunity to benefit from an appreciative global audience using other content media, such as podcasting, photo blogging, or vodcasting.

WHYVILLE

For younger students, Whyville (www.whyville.net) is a free but not open-source online community where 1.7 million children and young teens ages 9-15 meet to discuss books and films in the city's Greek theater, compete at checkers, go on art treasure hunts, and participate in a host of other activities. More than just a social network, Whyville is an educational tool sponsored by various entities including NASA (National Aeronautics and Space Administration) and designed to engage children in all types of activities that will support their understanding in real life. (Solomon 67)

Numedeon, Inc. launched Whyville in 1999 as a virtual city, engages young people in constructive educational activities while promoting socially responsible behavior. It is an outgrowth of the company's extensive research and practical experience related to learner-centered, hands-on, inquiry-based education. Inside Whyville, citizens learn about art history, science, journalism, civics, economics, and so much more. Whyville works directly with the Getty, NASA, the School Nutrition Association, and Woods Hole Oceanographic Institution (to name just a few) to bring incredible educational content to kids in an incredibly engaging manner.

MASTERYMAZE

The goal of MasteryMaze (http://www.masterymaze.com/) is to combine content management with a little social networking to create a space on the web where teachers and students can work together. It provides an online location to share and collaborate with blogs, podcasts, vodcasts, and wikis.

SAFETY AND SECURITY OF SOCIAL NETWORKS

The extensive sociological work of Danah Boyd, a University of Berkeley-based social scientist, provides some important insights into social networks. Boyd argues that there have been more articles published on predators than actual reported incidents online. Boyd equates profiles on MySpace with public display of identity. Comments from friends provide a channel for feedback and affection, in which there is an element of reciprocity. "When friends comment on someone's profile or photo," says Boyd, "They expect [their comments] to be reciprocated." Though many of these relationships are shallow, Boyd argues that the process plays an important role in how teens learn the rules of social life and cope with issues such as status, respect, gossip, and trust." (Tapscott 48, 49)

Most teenagers claim they are taking steps to protect themselves online from the most obvious areas of risk. A new survey shows that many youth actively manage their personal information as they perform a balancing act between keeping some important pieces of information confined to their network of trusted friends and, at the same time, participating in a new, exciting social network on a wider scale.

A survey by the Pew Internet and American Life Project suggests that today's teens face potential risks associated with online life. Some 32% of online teenagers and 43% of social-networking teens have been contacted online by complete strangers and 17% of online teens, and 31% of social networking teens have "friends" on their social network profile whom they have personally never met. Thirty-two percent of online teens have been contacted online by a complete stranger while profile-owning teens are much more likely to have been contacted. Nearly two-thirds (65%) of teens who had been contacted by a stranger ignored or deleted the contact. (Teens)

While social networking seems omnipresent in the lives of most tweens and teens outside of school, most school districts are cautious about its use in school and schools have policies against their use.

A recent survey revealed:

- 92 percent of the school districts require parents and/or students to sign an Internet Use Policy.
- 98 percent of the districts use software to block access to inappropriate sites.

- 84 percent of the districts have rules against online chatting in school.
- 81 percent of the districts have rules against instant messaging in school.
- 62 percent of the districts have rules against participating in bulletin boards or blogs.
- 60 percent prohibit sending and receiving e-mail in school.
- 52 percent specifically prohibit any use of social networking sites in school.

Despite the rules, there is some officially sanctioned, educationally packaged social networking occurring in schools. Almost 69 percent say they have student Web site programs. Nearly half, (49 percent) say their schools participate in online collaborative projects with other schools, and almost as many (46 percent) claim that, their students participate in online pen pal or other international programs. More than a third (35 percent) say their schools and/or students maintain blogs, either officially or in the context of instruction. More than 22 percent say their classrooms are involved in creating or maintaining wikis.

Many school districts also use social networking for professional purposes. For example, 27 percent say their schools participate in a structured teacher/principal online community. Interestingly, districts that report that their parents are influential in technology decision making are more active in social networking (71 percent vs. 59 percent in districts with low parental influence). (Teens)

DELETING ONLINE PREDATORS ACT

The Deleting Online Predators Act (DOPA) is a piece of legislation aimed at regulating media content. It provides via Universal Service Fund, a federal mandate to install blocking software on all public computers. Thus far, it has not become law. This act would amend the Communications Act of 1934 to require schools and libraries that receive universal service support to enforce a policy that:

1.   Prohibits access to a commercial social networking Web site or chat room unless used for an educational purpose with adult supervision; and
2.   Protects against access to visual depictions that are obscene, child pornography, or harmful to minors.

This act also allows an administrator, supervisor, or other authorized person to disable such a technology protection measure during use by an adult, or by minors with adult supervision, to enable access for educational purposes. (H.R. 1120)

Most school libraries already have filters on incoming Internet access due to the Children's Internet Protection Act (CIPA). Opponents of the bill point out that the language of the DOPA bill would extend such filtering to include Web sites based on specific technologies rather than specific content, including Web sites based on those technologies that are used for educational purposes.

In response to this proposed DOPA legislation, the American Library Association embraces the stand as best stated by Robert Doyle of the Illinois Library Association.

> *"If people were better informed about social networking sites and knew and used basic Internet safety tips, the cloud of fear may decline."*
> (Stephen)

SUMMARY

Online social networking is much like traditional, face-to-face networking except it has removed the time and location barrier and added more tools in which to communicate. Like many other tools that began as a purely social technology, educators are now able to take that technology and apply it to classroom teaching and learning as well as use it for professional development and communications.

Currently the most flexible and powerful site that educators can join or establish a social network themselves is the Ning Web site (http://www.ning.com/). Educators can easily establish a social network around any curriculum subject, topic, or interest area using the Ning site.

While educators need to stay abreast of all legislation pertaining to the use of the Internet, special care and constant supervision need to be taken at all times to protect the safety of young people online as well as protecting the privacy and security of all Internet users.

Chapter 14

MULTI-USER VIRTUAL ENVIRONMENTS

VALUE OF VIRTUAL WORLD IN EDUCATION

Using online gaming and virtual worlds in educational settings opens the doors for new possibilities in teaching and learning. Online games, if done right, can become a powerful tool to encourage groups to collaborate and work together. With the growth of the Internet came the growth of the desire to connect. People all over the world wanted to reach out and meet people from places they could never visit. In addition to the growth of the Internet and connectivity, the increased structure and power of computers also encouraged the development and growth of virtual worlds.

A virtual world learner can experiment, plan, solve problems, negotiate, collaborate, evaluate, learn from mistakes, take risks, while acquiring a wide range of life and employability skills, and improve self-esteem and learning skills. Learners can interact with environments and personalities in ways that can be difficult to manage for a large group in traditional training.

Using the virtual world for education has significant potential to foster constructivist learning. Putting students in contact with other students in an immersive environment challenges them to figure problems out for themselves, without explicit learning objectives and assessment.

Virtual worlds hold significant potential for a learner-led-rather than an outcome-based-model of exploration and knowledge development.

 Virtual learning contributes most to traditional learning when the subject matter is best learned through exploration and role-playing. One of the key values of a simulation/game is the ability for the participant to make meaningful choices — that is, to explore.

Value is added to online simulation when the participants are geographically dispersed. Virtual worlds can provide different types of activities than are available face-to-face. These online experiences can be extremely effective tools in developing teambuilding skills. It is possible to design activities that cannot be completed by a single player; a group must work together to strategize, develop a solution, maximize the various talents of the team members, and execute their plan together in order to succeed.

Possibilities of using massively multiplayer educational gaming applications across disciplines could include:

- Immersing in reading, writing, listening, and speaking
- Studying foreign language and culture
- Developing leadership and management skills
- Practicing strategies and applying knowledge.

TYPES OF WEB 2.0 EDUCATIONAL GAMES AND VIRTUAL WORLDS

The types of Web 2.0 educational games fall into five basic groups. Common acronyms used in describing these online, educational gaming includes:

1. MUD - Multi-User Domain
2. MOO - Multi-User Object Oriented
3. MUSE - Multi-User Simulated Environment
4. MUSH - Multi-User Simulated Hallucination
5. MUVE - Multi-User Virtual Education

The genre of a video game describes its basic style of game play. Modern educational games have grown so complex and sophisticated that they rarely fit into a single genre, but can contain elements of several.
The major genres include:

- Puzzle
- Adventure
- Sports
- Racing
- Role-Playing Game (RPG)
- Real Time Strategy (RTS)
- Simulation
- Massive Multiplayer Online Game (MMOG) & Massive Multiplayer Online Role Playing Games (MMORPG)

CLASSROOM APPLICATION OF SIMULATED ONLINE GAMES

STOCK-TRAK

Stock-Trak (http://www.stocktrak.com/) is the Web's leading provider of educational and challenging stock simulations for colleges, high schools, and the investing public. Stock-Trak provides its innovative stock market investing software and virtual stock market game platform to over 800 professors, with over 40,000 college students, and nearly 200,000 high school and middle school students worldwide.

TRENDIO

Trendio (http://www.trendio.com/) is the first current events stock exchange online simulation program. Trendio is a community-based site that makes it possible for students to visualize trends in the media and try to predict what will make the headlines tomorrow. In this environment students try to identify trends in businesses to invest in.

Instead of buying stock in companies with real money, users buy stock in certain news subjects with fake money. Words available include those from the world of politics, sport, and entertainment. The more the word appears in the news, the higher the value of the stock. Currently, the site uses about 3,000 online internet sources to gauge the value of each word. Users start with 10,000 Trendillions (currency of Trendio) in play money.

SIMCITY

SimCity (http://simcitysocieties.ea.com/) is a simulation and city-building personal computer game, first released in 1989. The original *SimCity* started a tradition of goal-centered, timed scenarios that could be won or lost depending on the performance of the player/mayor. The original cities were based on real world cities and attempted to re-create their general layout.

In SimCity the player(s) can mark land as being zoned as commercial, industrial, or residential, add buildings, change the tax rate, and build a power grid, transportation systems, and many other actions, in order to enhance the city. The player may face disasters including: flooding, tornadoes, fires, and earthquakes.

While most scenarios either take place in a fictional timeline or have a city under siege by a fictional disaster, a handful of available scenarios are based on actual historical events.

A series of upgrades and versions have evolved and creative educators have found multiple uses for the simulation activities within their curriculum. Since the release of SimCity, similar simulation games have been released focusing on different aspects of reality such as business simulation in capitalism.

SimCity Societies (http://simcitysocieties.ea.com) is the latest release in the SimCity franchise. The game integrates a social and cultural modeling component. Characteristics of each user-run SimCity are determined by the user through development of six social, cultural, and economic factors: productivity, prosperity, creativity, spirituality, authority, and knowledge.

The National Engineers Week Future City Competition (http://www.futurecity.org/) uses SimCity 4 Deluxe software. This program is developed to help seventh and eighth grade students discover and foster interests in math, science, and engineering. In a semester-long project, middle school students from across the U.S. use engineering principles to design and build cities of the future with a focus on self-sufficient water systems. Regional competition winners travel to Washington, D.C. to vie for the grand prize, a week at Space Camp.

HEALTH AND DISASTER SCENARIOS

Publichealthgames.com (http://www.publichealthgames.com/) is a portal for all games that have a public health message. These online simulations provide users with the ability to practice a public health scenario as often as needed. The Center for Disease Control and Prevention is funding this series of computer games to help prepare health workers and other first responders facing bioterrorism attacks, nuclear accidents, and pandemics. Besides preparing the healthcare workers for various scenarios, they can also provide an overview of different public crises for students considering careers in health care and public service.

MASSIVE MULTIPLAYER ONLINE GAME (MMOG) APPLICATIONS

Entropia Universe (www.project-entropia.com) or (www.entropiauniverse.com) was founded by actor and director Jon Jacobs and is run by Swedish software company MindArk. (Vossen 278) The Entropia Universe is more than a futuristic game since it is for real with real people, real activities, and a real cash economy in a massive online universe. This Real Cash Economy means that the Entropia Universe currency, the PED, has a fixed exchange rate with the US dollar, where 10 PED = 1US dollar.

Quest Atlantis (QA) (http://www.questatlantis.org), designed by the Center for Research on Learning & Technology at Indiana, is a learning and teaching project that uses a 3D multi-user environment to immerse children, ages 9-12, in educational tasks. It allows users to travel to virtual places to perform educational activities (known as Quests), talk with other users and mentors, and build virtual personae.

A Quest is curricular task designed to be entertaining yet educational. Each Quest is connected to local academic standards and to the team's commitments. Completing Quests requires that members participate in real-world, socially and academically meaningful activities, such as conducting environmental studies, researching other cultures, calculating frequency distributions, analyzing newspaper articles, interviewing community members, and developing action plans. (Quest)

Activeworlds Inc. (http://www.activeworlds.com/) provides software products and online services that permit users to enter, move about and interact with others in a computer generated, three-dimensional virtual environment using the Internet.
Active Worlds for Educators (http://www.activeworlds.com/edu/index.asp) in response to the growing demand from educators launched the virtual world of The Active Worlds Educational Universe (AWEDU) (http://www.activeworlds.com/edu/awedu.asp). The AWEDU is a unique educational community that makes the Active Worlds technology available to educational institutions, teachers, students, and individual programs in a focused setting. Using this community, educators are able to explore new concepts, learning theories, creative curriculum design, and discover new paradigms in social learning.

In addition to over 80 educational worlds available in the AWEDU, the online community includes educational worlds in the main Active Worlds Universe where classes are taught, experiments performed and meetings are held.

SECONDLIFE

Second Life (SL) (http://secondlife.com/) is an online 3D role-playing site created by San Francisco-based Linden Lab. SecondLife provides a three-dimensional virtual world that is built and owned by its residents. Users can build a house or a business, and can buy, sell, and trade with other residents. The SecondLife Marketplace currently supports monthly transactions valued at millions of U.S. dollars. The actual SL currency is the *Linden dollar,* which can be converted to and from U.S. dollars at an online exchange. The exchange rate fluctuates and is determined by money supply, but it hovers around one U.S. dollar worth approximately 275 Linden Dollars. (Vossen 276)

The SL virtual world imitates the real world. It consists of interlinked regions that contain land, water, and sky. Each region has an area of 65,536 Second Life square meters. SL residents often refer to regions as sims (short for simulators). The entire Second Life world is divided into areas that can include any number of regions governed by a given set of rules. A separate area called Teen grid is reserved for SL members between the ages of 13 and 17. Members in that age group are not allowed into the main adult area, and vice versa. (Rymaszewski 8)

Linden Lab is testing a new age identification system that will further secure and separate the adult content from teens. Schools districts that lock down their desktops with filters policies will likely face challenges with updating clients on SecondLife. Therefore, ports often need to be opened on firewalls to allow traffic to flow to the clients as well.

Almost all the objects in Second Life are created or built from solids (30 geometric shapes) called prims. Each region can support 15,000 prims (plus a reserve of around

10% to let it handle moving objects). (Rymaszewski 10, 11).

COMMON TERMS IN SECOND LIFE

- Avatar - A digital representation of a person having the ability to run, jump, fly, chat, instant-message and more with others they meet.
- Islands - Places avatars visit. Islands are bought and designed by individuals and organizations.
- In-world - Is what is happening within SecondLife, as opposed to the real, physical world outside of Second Life.
- Linden dollar (L$) - Second Life's virtual currency, which can be exchanged for U.S. dollars.
- Lindex - Second Life's currency exchange.
- Machinima - A form of filmmaking that uses computer game technology to shoot films in the virtual reality using a game engine.
- Orientation Island - First stop where Second Life newbies can learn the basics.
- Resident - Those with an active presence in Second Life.
- SL- Second Life.
- Teleport (or TP) - How avatars move instantly from spot to spot.
- V-commerce - Doing business in virtual worlds.
- V-product - What you buy or sell in virtual worlds.

One of the first things users face in Second Life is how to move from one location to another. If they have Second Life installed on their hard drive, clicking on the map link, will automatically teleport you to that location. However, the fastest way to move from one location to another is by a

direct teleport link using a link called a SL URL
(http://slurl.com/).

In addition to allowing customized control over mapping
locations in Second Life, SL URLs also provides a better
experience for Web users who do not have Second Life.
Instead of getting an error when clicking on Web links that
begin with "secondlife," visiting a SL URL link gives
potential new users a chance to sign up.

To generate SL URLs to use with Second Life, a
convenient SL URL Builder is located at
http://slurl.com/build.php.

GROUP COLLABORATION

One of the best features of SecondLife is the way it allows
users to collaborate with other residents. Together, they can
work on bigger and more complex projects, build on each
other's strengths, and make things that they might not be
able to on their own.

There are four options for collaborative building.

1. Modify Rights – Once you grant someone modify rights,
    they will be able to edit anything you own, anywhere in
    the world.
2. Group Land – When building with other people, it can
    be a good idea to form a group and deed land to that
    group. Group land will let you collaborate with other
    users on larger guilds. To link your objects together you
    will need to transfer ownership to one person and have
    that person link the objects. To do that, you have to play
    with asset permissions.

3. Asset permissions – are set in the General tab of the Build window. They define how future owners of the object (or copies of that object) may use it
4. Group deeding – Deeding an object means the transfer of ownership of an object to another group. Group deeding may cause the object not to work properly if it is a scripted object since many scripts rely upon the object being owned by a single owner. (Rymaszewski 150-152)

LSL stands for Linden Scripting language. It lets you add behaviors and interactivity to objects inside Second Life. Scripting is just another word for programming, so in learning about LSL you will end up learning about programming as well.

MEDICAL USES OF SECOND LIFE

Medical schools and health departments have also started using virtual worlds. A University of California psychiatrist developed a virtual psych ward echoing with disembodied voices to help caregivers understand schizophrenia better. Stanford University doctors built virtual operating and emergency rooms to train young doctors. Britain's National Health Service constructed an entire virtual hospital. Individual practitioners, meanwhile, are discovering virtual worlds on their own. Some therapists have started using virtual worlds to treat patients for a host of problems, in both their real and virtual lives. After meeting other health-care professionals in Second Life, Lawrence Whitehurst, a family doctor in Culpeper, Va., founded the Second Life Medical Association (Stein).

Before practicing medicine on real patients, nursing students at Tacoma Community College, in Washington, get to practice on virtual ones in the computer-generated world of Second Life. John Miller, a nursing instructor at Tacoma played the role of the patient, directing his avatar to lie on a hospital bed in the virtual emergency room. The avatars of two of his students, both of whom were participating remotely, treated the patient. Mr. Miller claimed that the virtual world gives nursing students a chance to practice their medical procedures on their own. It does not replace traditional learning or the live simulations at the college, but it does provide another method of practice *(Carnevale).*

Other medical communities are reaching out to SecondLife to help meet the needs of the public. The Centers for Disease Control and Prevention tested a small *office* in virtual world Second Life *staffed* by Hygeia Philo, an avatar named after the Greek goddess of health, and is now planning a bigger, permanent presence.
The American Cancer Society has an elaborate "island" offering virtual lectures by avatar doctors, support group meetings, and other activities. The March of Dimes is building a virtual neonatal intensive-care unit to warn about the dangers of preterm births. The National Library of Medicine is helping fund HealthInfo Island, where users can get reliable medical information on SecondLife (Stein).

UNIVERSITY AND PROFESSIONAL DEVELOPMENT USES OF SECOND LIFE

Reaching out to the academic world, Second Life launched an initiative for colleges and universities interested in using the grid as a pedagogical tool. Campus: Second Life (http://lindenlab.com/pressroom/releases/04_09_20) is available for use in college-level coursework including architecture, game design, sociology, and media studies. Faculty and students are able to integrate into the existing Second Life world community, or work together on unique private "islands."

K-12 USES OF SECOND LIFE

Second Life presents a novel and exciting way to engage students in distance learning. If you have spent time in Second Life, you will no doubt see a broad potential in the environment as well as aspects that may present challenges.

Many educational projects for young people are already on SecondLife Teen (http://teen.secondlife.com/) and others are in production. Kidz Connect (http://www.kidzconnect.org/), Global Kids' Digital Media Initiative (http://www.globalkids.org/), and The Schome Park Project (http://www.schome.ac.uk) are some of the more exemplar programs.

Kidz Connect is a program in Teen Second Life that connects young people in different countries via media art, performance, and creative collaboration within virtual worlds of Second Life. The project provides a contrast in the customs and languages of each city, teaching the students about different places. The participants learned a different assortment of skills throughout this project such as digital storytelling, live visual performance, improvisational theatre, soundscaping, sound recording and manipulation, video editing, live video streaming, collaborative performance, video conferencing, 3D modeling in Second Life, and programming (Second Life object scripting). (Wagner)

Global Kids' Digital Media Initiative (DMI) (http://www.globalkids.org/) is a series of interrelated programs designed to encourage and support teenagers in thinking critically about the role of digital media in their lives, promote constructive use of new media forms, and document their experiences. Within the program, Global Kids is using contests, online dialogues, a virtual world, podcasts, a blog, machinima, and other venues to gather valuable feedback and views from young people about their relationship with emerging media.

The Schome Park Project (http://www.schome.ac.uk/) is using an island in the Teen Grid of Second Life alongside a wiki and forum to develop thinking about schome (not school – not home – schome – the education system for the information age). While the schome community includes members of all ages from all around the world, the Schome Park Project focuses on working with 13 to 17 year olds. Current students come from the UK, the USA and the Falkland Islands.

EDUCATIONAL RESOURCES FOR USING SECONDLIFE IN THE CLASSROOM

Linden Lab has several people with academic backgrounds working full-time to support the use of Second Life for educational, academic, and "serious" applications. Educators can contact them directly with general questions about using the system, setting up islands, connecting with colleagues currently working in Second Life or contractors to help build projects. The education specialists maintain a wiki containing an official resource for educators in Second Life (http://www.simteach.com/wiki/index.php?title=Second_Life_Education_Wiki).

A team of Australian educators also maintains a similar resource. The Second Life in Education Wiki (http://sleducation.wikispaces.com/) provides a range of resources for educators who are interested in exploring the use of virtual worlds, in particular Second Life, in teaching and learning.

Linden Lab maintains an active Educators Mailing List (SLED) to keep interested individuals alerted to educational opportunities and events in Second Life. You can be added to this mailing list by filling out the form at (https://lists.secondlife.com/cgi-bin/mailman/listinfo/educators). In addition, they have a special mailing list for educators working with Teens (13-17yrs old) – SLEDT (https://lists.secondlife.com/cgi-bin/mailman/listinfo/educatorsandteens).

An in-world resource for educational technology worth investigating is the Edtech Island at http://slurl.com/secondlife/EdTech/114/76/25.

The International Society for Technology in Education (ISTE) Second Life Island (http://slurl.com/secondlife/ISTE%20Island/93/83/30) provides a venue for educators to network and learn from each other about real-life education opportunities and best practices in Second Life. ISTE holds regular meetings for educators and administrators in Second Life to discuss preplanned topics, such as preteen social networks.

SECOND LIFE AND PEOPLE WITH DISABILITIES

Popular media sources are beginning to report the impact that Second Life has had on those with disabilities. In a CBS News clip on November 28, 2007 entitled "New Life in Cyberspace" (Smith) brought this issue to the forefront of public awareness as she highlighted specific cases of the new lease on life people with disabilities gained from participating in Second Life.

Nov 13, 2007, the major news cable television network CNN announced their plans of entering Linden Lab's MMORPG virtual society. SecondLife hopes to understand what is making news in the new territory. CNN set up a SL presence and encourage SecondLife residents to submit reports to its virtual I-Report hub. When Second Life residents observe an in-world event they consider newsworthy, they can take snapshots, shoot video, or write a report about the event and submit to CNN. The CNN Blog covering news on second life can be consulted at http://secondlife.blogs.cnn.com/.

SLOODLE

Sloodle (http://www.sloodle.org/) is an Open Source project which aims to develop and share useful, usable, desirable tools for supporting education in virtual worlds, making teaching easier. The Sloodle project hopes to develop sound pedagogies for teaching across web-based and 3D virtual learning environments by integrating Second Life multi-user virtual environment and the Moodle learning-management system. You can find more details on the project and technical information on the development status on the Sloodle Wiki (http://slisweb.sjsu.edu/sl/index.php/Sloodle_Home_Page).

SUMMARY

As the early adapters move into the use of Multi-User Virtual Environments *and* SecondLife, other educators stand back and wonder if this is just a passing phase or if it will have lasting value to help students achieve their educational objectives, goals, and standards.

One thing that has been noted is that the early adapters seem to agree that using the virtual world for education does have significant potential to foster constructivist learning. Virtual worlds help students move to learner-led-rather than an outcome-based-model of exploration and knowledge development.

Many of the fears of using SecondLife with students were removed when SecondLife established a separate Teen section that no adults can enter. Linden Lab has provided a number of educators who prepare resources for teachers exploring the possibility of setting up a presence on SecondLife for their classes. Those resources combined with educators who have already established a virtual presence will help guide educators who are considering using SL resources for their own classrooms to meet their curricular needs.

Chapter 15

WEB 2.0 REAL-TIME COMMUNICATIONS

FEATURES OF WEB 2.0 COMMUNICATION

Web 2.0 provides a number of free and inexpensive real-time communication tools. The transmission technology for delivery of voice communications is known as Voice over Internet Protocol (VoIP). VoIP systems usually interface with the traditional public switched telephone network (PSTN) to allow for transparent phone communications worldwide. VoIP can be a benefit for reducing communication and infrastructure costs by routing phone calls over existing data networks and avoiding duplicate network systems.

Many of these Web 2.0 communication tools have been combined with other APIs to make extremely helpful Mashups. Internet communications surpasses the telephone and printing press with its openness and participatory features. These tools help keep all participants informed, up-to-date, and contributing. Web 2.0 makes the Internet more personalized than any other form of communication.

Web 2.0 communications allows the masses to communicate with each other without the oversight of governments or corporations. This has created an environment where ideas and freedom is allowed to flow unrestricted, but it has also caused some serious concerns when this freedom is used in a destructive manner.

One of the key problems with Web 2.0 is dependence. If your connection should go down, how will you access the information that you come to depend on? Because many web services are offered free of charge, they may not be secure, and hackers could easily target them.

WEB 2.0 COMMUNICATION PROGRAMS

SKYPE

Skype (http://www.skype.com/) offers free global telephony and unlimited voice calls with its next-generation peer-to-peer software. Many claim that Skype calls have better sound quality than a regular land phone and are highly secure, with end-to-end encryption. This simple software offers several features, including SkypeOut calling from Skype to regular and mobile phones worldwide, conference calling, and secure file transferring.

Niklas Zennström and Janus Friis founded Skype in 2003. The Skype Group, which was acquired by eBay in September 2005, has headquarters in Luxembourg, with offices in London, Tallinn, Prague, Tartu, and San Jose, California. It is now available in 28 languages and is used in almost every country around the world. Skype generates revenue through its offerings such as making and receiving calls to and from landline and mobile phones, as well as voicemail and call forwarding. Additional features include instant messaging, file transfer, short message service, video conferencing, and its ability to circumvent firewalls. Skype has relationships with a growing network of hardware and software providers.

Recently, Skype and Logitech, the world's leading manufacturer of webcams, announced a collaboration to deliver a new benchmark of high quality video calls over the Internet. Logitech's new webcam drivers are especially tuned to recognize callers who have this latest version of Skype software.

To begin using Skype, users merely need to download the software from (http://www.skype.com/), choose a Skype name, check that their microphone and speakers are on, make a free test call, find friends who use Skype, and start making calls. To begin talking or chatting with any Skype contact simply double-click on their Skype name.

Making a video call using Skype requires a webcam in addition to a headset or speakers and microphone. Users merely need to install the software for the webcam and plug in the webcam to the computer. Skype will automatically detect the webcam and offer a way to test the webcam to ensure everything is working correctly. Once that is done, any Skype call can include video.

To include multiple Skype contacts in the same call, users can simply click the conference button in the Skype window and add the desired parties. Skype can conference up to five people in a call on any computer and up to ten people in one call if the people on the call are using a PC with an Intel Duo Core Processor.

Telephone calls can be made from within Skype to land line or mobile phone numbers starting at approximately $.02 per minute using SkypeOut. Having a Skype phone number offers convenience to a user's contacts that are not on Skype. For approximately $30 per year, anyone can obtain a SkypeIn phone number with the area code of choice that will allow contacts outside the Skype network to call directly into Skype. Users can also set up Skype Voicemail so people can leave messages when they are not available.

TWITTER

Twitter (http://twitter.com/) is a community of friends and strangers from around the world sending updates about moments in their lives. Twitter is a combination of a free social networking and micro-blogging service that allows users to send updates via SMS (Short Message Service), instant messaging, email, to the Twitter Web site, or any of the multitudes of Twitter applications and Mashups (http://www.usrbingeek.com/a/000902.php) now available.

With Twitter users can tell people what they are doing all day long with short text-based updates, or 'tweets' of up to 140 characters long posted to the Twitter Web site, short message service, instant messaging, email, or an application such as Twitterrific (http://www.apple.com/downloads/macosx/email_chat/twitterrific.html). Twitterrific is a Mac OS X client that was created by The Iconfactory (http://iconfactory.com/software/twitterrific) that lets users view in real time "twitters" or micro-blog posts on the Twitter Web site as well as publish their own. Twitteroo (http://rareedge.com/twitteroo/) lets you send Twitter tweets from your desktop computer.

Unlike most normal social networks, Twitter does not require the use of a computer since updates can also be sent using a normal mobile phone. Twits can be used to increased readership to your blog, by sending a message that includes links to sites, other members, or anything you find interesting. Bloggers can use twitter as an interactive tool to keep readers up-to-date on the latest posts, news, or happenings, while also driving new readers and reaching a wider audience.

Every time a tweet is sent out, all the followers of that user will see it. Unlike blogs, Twitter is a real time broadcasting medium.

GOOGLE TALKS

GoogleTalk (http://www.google.com/talk/) Google Talk allows voice and video calls between personal computers, file transfers, and voicemail. Users can archive voice chats in Gmail, and obtain chat and email notifications.

GoogleTalk is also an instant messaging tool and that will allow users to view YouTube videos and Picasa Web Albums. It communicates with other clients that support the standard XMPP protocol. Therefore, you can chat with others who have iChat, AIM and several other chat clients. (Carey 72)

The Google Talk Gadget brings chat to the user's desktop. The Talk client is a Web-based module that can be embedded directly into an iGoogle page (the Google Personalized Homepage) or into a person's own Web site, complete with contact list and online status indicators for their friends. New chats will appear directly on the page. Google Talk Gadget can archive chats like Google Talk.

No matter where a user goes, all he has to do is login to his Google account, and there is the talk gadget. If a user has a Web page or blog, he can put the Google Talk Gadget in those places as well, so his visitors can sign in and start instant messaging right from that page. Like most other gadgets, the Web site creator can do this by merely pasting a single line of code into the Web page.
Another feature of GoogleTalk is that it looks and feels the same on a Linux desktop as on a Windows laptop, and on

Macs, as well. Therefore, users are able to move from platform to platform with ease.

EYEJOT

Eyejot (http://www.eyejot.com/) is a client-free online video messaging platform ideal for educational, personal, and business communications. It offers users the ability to create and receive video messages in a self-contained, spam-free environment. Users can start using Eyejot immediately using any browser, on any platform without downloading special software. The recipient receives a friendly email message telling them they have a new video message, and they can watch it with a single click. No registration required.

Eyejot offers people the ability to communicate easily and more naturally with one another through video while taking advantage of email's ability of working across geographies and time zones, and eliminating spam from the equation. Without facial expressions and gestures, readers can interpret email differently from what the writer had intended. With Eyejot e-mail contacts will not have any trouble understanding what is meant. Readers will be able to see the sender's energy, passion, concern, interest, excitement, and humor. They'll both see and hear it.

VIDEO CONFERENCING SERVICES

FLASHMEETING

FlashMeeting (http://flashmeeting.open.ac.uk/) is an application based on the Adobe Flash plug in and Flash Media Server. Running in a standard Web browser window, it allows a group of people to video conference from anywhere in the world with only an Internet connection. Typically, a meeting is pre-booked by a registered user.

The FlashMeeting server returns a URL, containing a unique password for the meeting. The 'booker' passes this information on to the people they wish to participate, who simply click on the link to enter into the meeting at the arranged time. During the meeting one person speaks (broadcasts) at a time. Other people can simultaneously contribute using text chat, the whiteboard, or emoticons while waiting for their turn to speak. A replay of the meeting is instantly available for those with the replay URL.

FlashMeeting has some advantages over other VOIP/Video Conferencing programs, the main one being no download is necessary, as all FlashMeetings take place through a host server. Organizations can purchase their own FlashMeeting server and not have to rely on the open servers. There are also bandwidth issues with some VOIP programs. If there are a high number of people in a Conference Call and the conversation allow many to speak at once, it can be a high demand on your computer memory.

ZOHO MEETING

Zoho Meeting (http://meeting.zoho.com/) is an online meeting service to show/share a desktop online, conduct Web meeting, or troubleshoot/provide remote assistance to your customers. All that is needed is a browser and an Internet connection for conducting a meeting. With Zoho Meeting, you can host live Web conferences and chat with all participants. You can edit, and share meeting online and join from anywhere with whomever you choose. You can also save the meeting and embed it inside Zoho Show, Zoho Notebook or any public Web page or blog.

GOTO MEETING

Citrix GoToMeeting (www.gotomeeting.com/) is a Web conferencing tool that allows participants to meet online rather than in a conference room. GoToMeeting allows anyone with a PC and Internet browser to host or attend an online meeting in seconds. Meeting organizers can start a meeting with one click or schedule future meetings in one-step. Meeting attendees do not need pre-loaded software or administrative privileges to participate, but can attend a meeting by simply clicking a URL sent from the meeting host. Once all invited attendees are in the meeting, the presenter can share any file or application on the desktop, change presenters, or give keyboard and mouse control to an attendee.

SUMMARY

With the increase of high-speed Internet and Voice Over Internet Protocol (VOIP), the level of communication and collaboration between professional educators and students has exploded. No longer are educators and students limited by distance and cost. With an Internet connection, a computer, or cell phone, users can be in constant contact for individual or group meetings – or just to share the happening of the moment.

APPENDIX A

National Educational Technology Standards for Students: The Next Generation
"What students should know and be able to do to learn effectively and
live productively in an increasingly digital world ..."

1. Creativity and Innovation
Students demonstrate creative thinking, construct knowledge, and develop innovative products and processes using technology. Students:
   a. apply existing knowledge to generate new ideas, products, or processes.
   b. create original works as a means of personal or group expression.
   c.. use models and simulations to explore complex systems and issues.
   d. identify trends and forecast possibilities.

2. Communication and Collaboration
Students use digital media and environments to communicate and work collaboratively, including at a distance, to support individual learning and contribute to the learning of others. Students:
   a. interact, collaborate, and publish with peers, experts or others employing a variety of digital environments and media.
   b. communicate information and ideas effectively to multiple audiences using a variety of media and formats.

c. develop cultural understanding and global awareness by engaging with learners of other cultures.

d. contribute to project teams to produce original works or solve problems.

3. Research and Information Fluency

Students apply digital tools to gather, evaluate, and use information. Students:

a. plan strategies to guide inquiry.

b. locate, organize, analyze, evaluate, synthesize, and ethically use information from a variety of sources and media.

c. evaluate and select information sources and digital tools based on the appropriateness to specific tasks.

d. process data and report results.

4. Critical Thinking, Problem-Solving & Decision-Making

Students use critical thinking skills to plan and conduct research, manage projects, solve problems and make informed decisions using appropriate digital tools and resources. Students:

a. identify and define authentic problems and significant questions for investigation.

b. plan and manage activities to develop a solution or complete a project.

c. collect and analyze data to identify solutions and/or make informed decisions.

d. use multiple processes and diverse perspectives to explore alternative solutions.

5. Digital Citizenship

Students understand human, cultural, and societal issues related to technology and practice legal and ethical behavior. Students:

   a. advocate and practice safe, legal, and responsible use of information and technology.

   b. exhibit a positive attitude toward using technology that supports collaboration, learning, and productivity.

   c. demonstrate personal responsibility for lifelong learning.

   d. exhibit leadership for digital citizenship.

6. Technology Operations and Concepts

Students demonstrate a sound understanding of technology concepts, systems and operations. Students:

   a. understand and use technology systems.

   b. select and use applications effectively and productively.

   c. troubleshoot systems and applications.

   d. transfer current knowledge to learning of new technologies.

APPENDIX B

RSS Feed Aggregators and Creators

RSS FEED AGGREGATORS (READERS)

Feed Reader or News Aggregator software allows you to grab the RSS feeds from various sites and display them for you to read and use. A variety of RSS Readers are available for different platforms. Popular feed readers include:

- Active Web Reader (Windows) <http://www.deskshare.com/awr.aspx>
- Apple Mail (Mac OS) < http://www.apple.com/macosx/features/mail.html>
- Amphetadesk (Windows, Linux, Mac) <http://www.disobey.com/amphetadesk/>
- Bloglines (Web based) <http://www.bloglines.com/>
- FeedReader (Windows) <http://www.feedreader.com/>
- FeedDemon (Windows) <http://www.newsgator.com/Individuals/FeedDemon/De fault.aspx>
- Google Reader (Web based) <http://www.google.com/reader/>
- Internet Explorer 7 (Windows) <http://www.microsoft.com/windows/products/winfamil y/ie/default.mspx>
- Juice (cross-platform) < http://juicereceiver.sourceforge.net/>
- Microsoft Outlook 2007 (Windows) <http://office.microsoft.com/en-us/outlook/default.aspx>
- NewsGator <http://www.newsgator.com/ >
- *Safari (Mac and Windows) <http://www.apple.com/safari/>

- Sage, a Firefox extension (cross-platform)
  <http://sage.mozdev.org/>
- Yahoo (Web based)
  <http://my.yahoo.com/s/about/rss/index.html>

RSS GENERATORS/CREATORS

Special software is necessary to create, edit, and publish RSS feeds. The most common ones include:
- FeedForAll (Windows and Mac)
  <http://www.feedforall.com/>
- FeedYes (Web based) <http://www.feedyes.com/>
- IceRocket Free RSS Builder (Web based) <
  http://rss.icerocket.com/>
- Online RSS Creator (Web based)
  <http://www.webreference.com/cgi-bin/perl/makerss.pl>
- RSS Feed Generator
  <http://www.rssfeedssubmit.com/rss-generator/>
- RSS Generator
  <http://www.freefeedgenerator.com/?hop=0>
- XML Feed Generator <http://www.makeafeed.com/>

Works Cited

"About Us." TeacherTube - Teach the World. 2007. 29
Dec. 2007 <http://www.teachertube.com/
about.php>.

Adobe. "Upgrading the Internet – Web 2.0." Weblog entry.
17 Nov. 2005. Interakt: Simplifying Web
Development. Adobe Co. 26 Dec. 2007
<http://www.interaktonline.com/Support/Articles/
Details/?id_art=39>.

Alexander, Bryan. "Web 2.0: A New Wave of Innovation
for Teaching and Learning?" EDUCAUSE Review
41.2 (Mar.-Apr. 2006): 32-44. 10 Sept. 2007
<http://www.educause.edu/ir/library/pdf/
erm0621.pdf>.

"All about RSS." Fegan Finder. 19 Feb. 2004. 11 Sept.
2007 <http://www.faganfinder.com/search/rss.php>.

Anderson, Paul. "What is Web 2.0? Ideas, technologies and
implications for education." JISC Technology &
Standards Watch. Feb. 2007. 19 Aug. 2007
<http://www.jisc.ac.uk/media/documents/
techwatch/tsw0701b.pdf>.

Bates, Mary Ellen. "Blog Searching with Technorati."
Online 31.4 (July-Aug. 2007). Academic Search
Elite. EBSCO. U of Wisconsin-Stout. 23 Nov. 2007
<http://ezproxy.lib.uwstout.edu:2170/ehost/
detail?vid=4&hid=112&sid=16a3107a-a>.

Bell, Ann. *Creating Digital Video in Your School.*
Worthington, OH: Linworth, 2005.

- - -. *Handheld Computers in Schools and Media Centers.*
Worthington, OH: Linworth, 2007.

Benzinger, Brian. "Back to School with the Class of Web
2.0." Weblog entry. 29 Sept. 2006. Solution Watch.
27 Aug. 2007 <http://www.solutionwatch.com/512/
back-to-school-with-the-class-of-web-20-part-1/>.

Boss, Suzie, and Krauss Jane. "Power of the Mashup: Combining Essential Learning with New Technology tools." Learning & Leading with Technology 35.1 (Aug. 2007): 12 - 17.

Branzburg, Jeffrey. "Use Google Maps Mashups in K-12 Education." TeachLEARNING. 15 May 2006. 3 Dec. 2007 <http://www.techlearning.com/story/showArticle.php?articleID=187002846>.

Breen, Christopher. "How to Create a Vodcast: Steps for Offering Video on Demand." Playlist. 26 July 2005. 26 Nov. 2007 <http://playlistmag.com/features/2005/07/howtovodcast/index.php>.

California Open Source Textbook Project. 2002. 29 Nov. 2007 <http://www.opensourcetext.org/>.

Carey, Chris, et al. An Educator's Guide To: Google Apps for Education. n.p.: FTC, 2007.

Carnevale, Dan. "To Save a Second Life." Weblog entry. 13 Nov. 2007. The Chronicle of Higher Education: The Wired Campus. 22 Dec. 2007 <http://chronicle.com/wiredcampus/article/2541/to-save-a-second-life>.

Casey, Michael E., and Laura C. Savastinuk. *Library 2.0: A Guide to Participatory Library Service*. Medford: Information Today, 2007.

Crawford, Walt. "Library 2.0 & 'Library 2.0.'" Cites & Insights 6.2 (Winter 2006): 1-32. 27 Aug. 2007 <http://citesandinsights.info/civ6i2.pdf>.

"Creating & Connecting: Research and Guidelines on Online Social and Educational Networking." National School Boards Association. July 2007. 19 Oct. 2007 <http://www.nsba.org/site/docs/41400/41340.pdf>.

Cross, Jay. "What is Informal Learning?" Weblog entry. 26 May 2006. Informal Learning Blog. 17 Dec. 2007 <http://informl.com/the-informal-learning-page/>.

Davis, Anne. "Rationale for Educational Blogging."
    Weblog entry. 7 Jan. 2007. EduBlog Insights. 23
    Nov. 2007 <http://anne.teachesme.com/2007/01/17/
    rationale-for-educational-blogging/>.
Deal, Ashley. "Podcasting: A Teaching with Technology
    White Paper." Research on Teaching with
    Technology. 4 June 2007. Carnegie Mellon U. 29
    Dec. 2007 <http://www.cmu.edu/teaching/
    resources/PublicationsArchives/
    StudiesWhitepapers/Podcasting_Jun07.pdf>.
Draggon, Maurice, et al. Emergy Internet Technology. n.p.:
    FTC, 2007.
D'Souza, Quentin. *Web 2.0 Ideas for Educators : a Guide
    to RSS and More*. Ver. 2.0 ed. Teaching Hacks.com.
    26 Oct. 2006. 5 Sept. 2007
    <http://www.teachinghacks.com/
    files//100ideasWeb2educators.pdf>.
Eisenberg, Anne. "Do the Mash (Even If You Don't Know
    All the Steps)." The New York Times 2 Sept. 2007.
    4 Dec. 2007 <http://www.nytimes.com/2007/09/02/
    technology/circuits/
    02novelties.html?_r=2&th&emc=th&oref=slogin&
    oref=slogin>.
Fichter, Darlene. "Intranet Applications for Tagging and
    Folksonomies." Online 30.3 (May-June 2006).
    Academic Search Elite. EBSCO. University of
    Wisconsin-Stout Library. 29 Sept. 2007
    <http://search.ebscohost.com/>.
Freedman, Terry. Coming of Age: An Introduction to the
    New World Wide Web. Ilford, England: Terry
    Freedman, LTD, 2006. 27 Aug. 2007
    <http://www.shambles.net/web2/comingofage/
    Coming_of_age_v1-2.pdf>.

- - -. "How to Create a Blogroll." Weblog entry. 24 Aug.
2007. Using & Teaching Educational Technology.
The Educational Technology Site: ICT in
Education. 21 Nov. 2007 <http://terry-
freedman.org.uk/artman/publish/article_1146.php>.

"Getting Started: A Guide for Using iPods for Teaching
and Learning." iPod in Education. May 2007.
Apple. 27 Sept. 2007 <http://images.apple.com/
education/products/ipod/
iPod_Getting_Started_Guide.pdf>.

Good, Robin. "Folksonomies: Tags Strengths,
Weaknessesand How to Make Them Work." Master
New Media. 1 Feb. 2006. 13 Sept. 2007
<http://www.masternewmedia.org/news/2006/02/
01/
folksonomies_tags_strengths_weaknesses_and.htm
#>.

Grosseck, Gabriela. Using Del.icio.us in Education. 30 Oct.
2007 <http://www.scribd.com/doc/212002/Using-
delicious-In-Education>.

Havenstein, Heather. Wiki Becomes Textbook in Boston
College Classroom. 15 Aug. 2007. ComputerWorld
Networking & Internet. 30 Nov. 2007
<http://www.computerworld.com/action/
article.do?command=viewArticleBasic&articleId=9
030802>.

Hinchcliffe, Dion. "The State of Web 2.0." Weblog entry. 2
Apr. 2006. Dion Hinchcliffe's Web 2.0 Blog. 26
Dec. 2007
<http://web2.socialcomputingmagazine.com/
the_state_of_web_20.htm>.

- - -. "Thinking in Web 2.0: Sixteen Ways." Weblog entry.
26 Feb. 2006. Dion Hinchcliffe's Web 2.0 Blog. 10
Sept. 2007
<http://web2.socialcomputingmagazine.com/
thinking_in_web_20_sixteen_ways.htm>.
"H.R. 1120, the Deleting Online Predators Act of 2007."
WashingtonWatch.com. 31 Dec. 2007
<http://www.washingtonwatch.com/bills/show/
110_HR_1120.html>.
"The Intellectual and Policy Foundations of the 21st
Century Skills Framework." Partnership for the 21st
Century Skills. 14 Oct. 2007. 30 Nov. 2007
<http://www.21stcenturyskills.org/route21/images/
stories/epapers/skills_foundations_final.doc>.
Kids Connect. 22 Dec. 2007 <http://zoomlab.org/wiki/
index.php?title=Kids_Connect>.
Kuhlmann, Tom. The Insider's Guide to Becoming a Rapid
E-Learning Pro. 2007. 11 Dec. 2007
<http://www.articulate.com/rapid-elearning/
downloads/
Insiders_Guide_To_Becoming_A_Rapid_E-
Learning_Pro.pdf>.
Lager, Marshall. "It's All Coming 2.0gether." CRM
Magazine Dec. 2007. 4 Dec. 2007
<http://www.destinationcrm.com/articles/
default.asp?ArticleID=7397>.
Lenhart, Amanda, and Mary Madden. "Social Networking
Web sites and Teens: An Overview." Pew Internet
& American Life Project. 3 Jan. 2007. 18 Dec.
2007 <http://www.pewinternet.org/pdfs/
PIP_SNS_Data_Memo_Jan_2007.pdf>.
- - -. "Teens, Privacy and Online Social Networks." Pew
Internet & American Life Project. 18 Apr. 2007. 18
Dec. 2007 <http://www.pewinternet.org/pdfs/
PIP_Teens_Privacy_SNS_Report_Final.pdf>.

"LibraryThing." Wikipedia. 6 Nov. 2007
     <http://en.wikipedia.org/wiki/LibraryThing>.
"Mashups and APIs." Scottish Institute for Excellence in
     Social Work Education. Jan. 2007. 4 Dec. 2007
     <http://www.sieswe.org/files/05_mashups.pdf>.
Mathes, Adam. "Folksonomies - Cooperative Classification
     and Communication Through Shared Metadata."
     adammathes.com. Dec. 2004. 13 Sept. 2007
     <http://www.adammathes.com/academic/computer-
     mediated-communication/folksonomies.html>.
Mejías, Ulises Ali. "Tag Literacy." Weblog entry. 26 Apr.
     2005. Ideant. 13 Sept. 2007
     <http://ideant.typepad.com/ideant/2005/04/
     tag_literacy.html>.
National Educational Technology Standards for Students:
     The Next Generation. Eugene, OR: International
     Society for Technology in Education, 2007. 9 Sept.
     2007 <http://www.iste.org/inhouse/nets/cnets/
     students/pdf/NETS_for_Students_2007.pdf>.
O'Reilly, Tim. "What Is Web 2.0: Design Patterns and
     Business Models for the Next Generation of
     Software." O'Reilly. 30 Sept. 2005. 19 Aug. 2007
     <http://www.oreillynet.com/pub/a/oreilly/tim/news/
     2005/09/30/what-is-web-20.html>.
Parry, David. "The Technology of Reading and Writing in
     the Digital Space: Why RSS is Crucial for a
     Blogging Classroom." Weblog entry. 1 Oct. 2006.
     Blogs for learning. 10 Sept. 2007
     <http://blogsforlearning.msu.edu/articles/
     view.php?id=6>.
Pick, Tom. "Backflip: A Dot-Com Survivor Story."
     Weblog entry. 29 June 2005. The
     WebMarketCentral Blog. 27 Dec. 2007
     <http://webmarketcentral.blogspot.com/2005/06/
     backflip-dot-com-survivor-story.html>.

Quest Atlantis. 31 Dec. 2007
<http://atlantis.crlt.indiana.edu/public/welcome.pl>.

Ramos, Miguel, and Dawn Gauthier. "Mash It Up!"
Searcher 15.6 (June 2006): 17-22. Academic Search
Elite. EBSCO. U of Wisconsin-Stout. 4 Dec. 2007
<http://search.ebscohost.com/>.

Rice, William H., IV. *Moodle E-Learning Course
Development: A Complete Guide to Successful
learning using Moodle.* Birmingham, UK: Packt,
2006.

Richardson, Wil. "Using RSS Enclosures in Schools."
Weblog entry. 1 Mar. 2005. Webblogg-ed: Learning
with the Read/Write Web. 26 Dec. 2007
<http://weblogg-ed.com/2005/using-rss-enclosures-
in-schools/>.

Richardson, Will. *Blogs, Wikis, Podcasts, and Other
Powerful Web Tools for Classrooms.* Thousand
Oaks, CA: Corwin, 2006.

- - -. "Using RSS Enclosures in Schools." Weblog entry. 1
Mar. 2005. Weblogg-ed. 1 Oct. 2007
<http://weblogg-ed.com/2005/using-rss-enclosures-
in-schools/>.

Rymaszewski, Michael, et al. *Second Life: The Official
Guide.* Indianapolis: Wiley, 2007.

Schmit, Dan. *Kidcast: Podcasting in the Classroom.* N.p.:
Intellilgenic.com, 2007.

Serim, Ferdi, and Kathy Schrock. "Nailing Digital Jelly to a
Virtual Tree: Tracking Emerging Technologies for
Learning." Learning & Leading with Technology
35.4 (Dec.-Jan. 2007): 12-116.

Shankland, Stephen. "Geotagging Links Photos to
Locales." ZDNet News. 4 Sept. 2007. 4 Dec. 2007
<http://news.zdnet.com/2100-9584_22-
6205734.html?tag=nl.e539>.

Smith, Tiffany L. Cataloging and You: Measuring the
Efficicacy of a Folksonomy for Subject Analysis.
31 Oct. 2007 <http://dlist.sir.arizona.edu/2061/01/
Smith_Updated.doc>.
Smith, Tracy. Interview. New Life in Cyberspace. CBS
News. 28 Nov. 2007. 22 Dec. 2007
<http://www.cbsnews.com/sections/i_video/
main500251.shtml?id=3547970n>.
Snipes, Phyllis R. "Folksonomhy vs. Minnie Earl and
Melville." Library Media Connection 25.7 (Apr.-
May 2007): 54-56.
"Social Networking for Teachers." WikiSpaces. 2007. 18
Dec. 2007
<http://socialnetworking4teachers.wikispaces.com/
>.
Solomon, Gwen, and Lynne Schrum. *Web 2.0 : New Tools,
New Schools*. Eugene, OR: International Society for
Technology in Education, 2007.
"SOS Children UK and the Wikimedia Foundation
Announce the Launch of the Wikipedia Selection
for Schools." Wikimedia Foundation. 29 May 2007.
30 Dec. 2007 <http://wikimediafoundation.org/
wiki/Press_releases/SOSChildrenUK2007>.
Stein, Rob. "Real Hope in a Virtual World."
WashingtonPost.com 6 Oct. 2007. 22 Dec. 2007
<http://www.washingtonpost.com/wp-dyn/content/
article/2007/10/05/AR2007100502391_pf.html>.
Stephen, Downes. Principles for Evaluating Web sites. 16
June 2005. 25 Aug. 2007 <http://www.downes.ca/
cgi-bin/page.cgi?post=4>.

Stephens, Michael. "Thoughtful Advocates: An ALA
    TechSource Interview with ILA's Robert Doyle."
    Weblog entry. 28 Feb. 2007. ALA TechSource. 18
    Dec. 2007 <http://www.techsource.ala.org/blog/
    2007/02/thoughtful-advocates-an-ala-techsource-
    interview-with-ilas-robert-doyle.html>.
Tapscott, Don, and Anthony D. Williams. *Wikinomics:
    How Mass Collaboration Changes Everything.* New
    York: Portfolio - Penguin, 2006.
Terdiman, Daniel. "Study: Wikipedia as Accurate as
    Britannica." CNET.com News. 15 Dec. 2005. 30
    Dec. 2007 <http://www.news.com/2100-1038_3-
    5997332.html>.
"The 2007 Horizon Report." The New Media Consortium.
    2007. 30 Dec. 2007 <http://www.nmc.org/pdf/
    2007_Horizon_Report.pdf>.
"Upgrading the Internet – Web 2.0." Interakt. 17 Nov.
    2005. Adobe. 10 Sept. 2007
    <http://www.interaktonline.com/Support/Articles/
    Details/?id_art=39>.
Valenza, Joyce. "Ten Reasons Why Your Next Pathfinder
    Should be a Wiki." Weblog entry. 20 June 2007.
    School Library Journal. 2 Dec. 2007
    <http://www.schoollibraryjournal.com/blog/
    1340000334/post/1620010962.html>.
Vander Wal, Thomas. "Wikipedia Folksonomy is a Mess
    with Collaborative Misunderstanding." Weblog
    entry. 29 Nov. 2007. 2 Dec. 2007
    <http://www.vanderwal.net/random/
    entrysel.php?blog=1949>.
Vossen, Gottfried, and Stephan Hagemann. *Unleashing
    Web 2.0: From Concepts to Creativity.* Burlington,
    MA: Elsevier, 2007.

Warlick, David F. <u>Classroom Blogging: AS Teacher's Guide to Blogs, Wikis, & Other Tools That Are Shaping a New Information Landscape</u>. Raleigh, N.C.: Landmark Project, 2007.

Wenzler, John. "LibraryThing and the Library Catalog: Adding Collective Intelligence to the OPAC." <u>San Francisco State University</u>. 7 Sept. 2007. 6 Nov. 2007 <http://online.sfsu.edu/~jwenzler/research/LTFL.pdf>.

"What Is Wikibooks." <u>Wikibooks</u>. 30 Nov. 2007. 2 Dec. 2007 <http://en.wikibooks.org/wiki/Wikibooks:What_is_Wikibooks>.

"Wikiversity:Archive/About." <u>Wikiversity</u>. 30 Dec. 2007 <http://en.wikiversity.org/wiki/About>.

Williams, Bard. *Educator's Podcast Guide*. Eugene, OR: International Society for Technology in Education, 2007.

Wojcicki, Esther. "Docs & Spreadsheets in the Classroom." <u>Google Teacher Academy</u>. 25 June 2007. 7 Dec. 2007 <http://www.google.com/educators/learning_materials/necc_docs_spreadsheets.pdf>.

Glossary

AAC - Short for *Advanced Audio Coding*, one of the audio compression formats. Audio format of Apple's iPhone, iPod, iTunes, and the format used for all iTunes Store.

AIFF - Short for *Audio Interchange File Format*, a common format for storing and transmitting sound. The standard audio format for Macintosh computers.

APA Style Format - American Psychological Association **(APA)** style is a widely accepted style of documentation.

API - Application Program Interface

Attribution – Licensing Requirement of Creative Commons that requires the use to the user must attribute the work in the manner specified by the author or licensor (but not in any way that suggests they endorse you or your use of the work).

Autopan - The region you are recording moves as you move the mouse.

Avatar - A digital representation of a person having the ability to run, jump, fly, chat, instant-message and more with others they meet.

Bibliophile – A lover of books, but especially for the qualities of the format.

Blog – Short for of *web log*. It is a Web site where entries are commonly displayed in reverse chronological order. "*Blog*" can also be used as a verb, meaning *to maintain or add content to a blog.*

Blogosphere - Blogosphere is a collective term encompassing all blogs and their interconnections. It is the perception that blogs exist together as a connected community or a social network.

Bookmarklets - An applet, a small computer application, stored as the URL of a bookmark in a web browser or as a hyperlink on a Web page.

Chicago Style Manual – A style guide for American English published by the University of Chicago Press, prescribing a writing style widely used in publishing.

Children's Internet Protection Act (CIPA) - One of a number of bills that the United States Congress has proposed in an attempt to limit children's exposure to pornography and other controversial material online.

Compression - Storing data in a format that requires less space than usual. It is particularly useful in communications because it enables devices to transmit or store the same amount of data in fewer bits.

Course management program (CMS) - A software system designed to help teachers by facilitate the management of educational courses for their students with course administration in a virtual learning environment (VLE).

Craigslist - A centralized network of online communities, featuring free classified advertisements and forums on various topics.

Creative Commons – A non-profit organization devoted to expanding the range of creative work available for others legally to build upon and share through a copyright licensing system.

Cross-fade - A video transition where the first video gradually fades into the second video.

CVS (Concurrent Versions System) - is an open-source version control system that keeps track of all work and all changes in a set of files, and allows several developers to collaborate.

Data Rate - The speed with which data can be transmitted from one device to another.

Data Type – In programming, classification of a particular type of information; a computer uses special internal codes to keep track of the different types of data it processes.

Discussion Board (Forum Discussion Board) – A web application for holding discussions and posting user generated content.

Deleting Online Predators Act (DOPA) - A bill brought before the United States House of Representatives requiring schools and libraries that receive E-rate funding to protect minors from online predators in the absence of parental supervision when using *Commercial Social Networking Web sites* and *Chat Rooms*.

Edtech Island- A free, open-access resource in SecondLife to support educators in the study and use of virtual world environments for teaching and learning.

Environmental noise - Displeasing human or machine created sound that disrupts the activity or happiness of human or animal life.

E-learning (Electronic learning or eLearning) - A general term used to refer to computer-enhanced learning. **eVideo -** a convergence of technologies to efficiently deliver high quality video over IP networks.

FTP (File Transfer Protocol) - Commonly used protocol for exchanging files over any TCP/IP based network to manipulate files on another computer on that network regardless of which operating systems are involved.

Feed Aggregator - Also known as a feed reader, news reader or simply as an aggregator which aggregates syndicated web content such as news headlines, blogs, podcasts, and vodcasts in a single location for easy viewing.

Feed Generator/Creator - Creates RSS/XML feed files for download and to include in your Web pages.

Feed Reader – Same as a Feed Aggregator.

Flickr - a Web 2.0 photo sharing Web site and web services suite, and an online community platform.

Fliction - This form has been coined "flicktion" (=flickr + fiction) which others have picked up as a way to use images and story together. A flickr group called Visual

Storytelling has created a visual form of story in which the entire tale must be told with only five images (and no text).

Folksonomy- Folksonomy (also known as collaborative tagging , social classification, social indexing, social tagging, and other names) is the practice and method of collaboratively creating and managing tags to annotate and categorize content.

GeoTagging - Geotagging, sometimes referred to as Geocoding, is the process of adding geographical identification metadata to various media such as Web sites, RSS feeds, or images.

Google Talk – Google communications systems that include Instant messaging, Gmail notifications, PC-to-PC voice calls, and File transfers.

HTML - Short for *HyperText Markup Language,* the authoring language used to create documents on the World Wide Web.

H.264 - H.264 is a standard for video compression. It is also known as MPEG-4 Part 10 or MPEG-4 AVC (for *Advanced Video Coding*).

ID3 - a metadata container most often used in conjunction with the MP3 audio file format. It allows information such as the title, artist, album, track number, or other information about the file to be stored in the file itself.

iGoogle - Formerly Google Personalized Homepage is a customizable homepage. Updates include the capability to add web feeds and Google Gadgets.

Information Silo - Applied to management systems where the focus is inward and information communication is vertical.

In-world - What is happening within SecondLife, as opposed to the real, physical world outside of Second Life.

Islands - Places on SecondLife are 65,536 square meters (about 16 acres) that are priced at $1,675 U.S. dollars that Avatars visit.

Keyframe (or key frame) - In filmmaking and animation it is the starting and ending points of any smooth transition.

LAME - LAME is a free software application used to encode audio into the MP3 file format.

Librarything.com - A social cataloging web application for storing and sharing personal library catalogs and book lists.

Linden dollar (L$) - Second Life's virtual currency, which can be exchanged for U.S. dollars.

Lindex - Second Life's currency exchange.

Listal - A social network where you can list and rate the things you love.

MMORPG (Massively multiplayer online role-playing game) - A genre of online computer role-playing games (CRPGs) in which a large number of players interact with one another in a virtual world.

MOO - Multi-User Object Oriented - A text-based online virtual reality system to which multiple users (players) are connected at the same time.

MP3 - The name of a type of file for MPEG, audio layer 3 and also a file extension. Layer 3 is one of three coding schemes (layer 1, layer 2 and layer 3) for the compression of audio signals.

MPEG-4 - A graphics and video lossy compression algorithm standard that is based on MPEG-1 and MPEG-2 and Apple QuickTime technology.

MUD (Multi-User Domain) - A multi-player computer game that combines elements of role-playing games, hack and slash style computer games and social chat rooms.

MUSE (Multi-User Simulated Environment) - Incorporate computer graphics, sound, simulation, and networks to simulate the experience of real-time interaction between multiple users in a shared three-dimensional virtual world.

MUSH (Multi-User Simulated Hallucination) - A text-based online social medium to which multiple users are connected at the same time.

MUVE (Multi-User Virtual Education) - Online, multi-user virtual environments, sometimes called virtual worlds. While this term has been used to refer to a change in MUDs, MOOs, and MMORPGs, it is most widely used to describe MMOGs that are not necessarily game-specific.

Machinima -A form of filmmaking that uses computer game technology to shoot films in the virtual reality using a game engine.

Marc cataloging - Formats are standards for the representation and communication of bibliographic and related information in machine-readable form.

Mashup - A web application that combines data and/or functionality from more than one source.

Metadata - Data about data. An item of metadata may describe an individual datum, or content item, or a collection of data including multiple content items.

MLA Format - An academic style guide published for the Modern Language Association of America, which provides guidelines for writing and documentation of research in the humanities, especially in English studies; the study of other modern languages and literatures.

Moblog - A blog published directly to the web from a phone or other mobile device.

Moodle - Moodle is a free software e-learning platform *(also known as a Course Management System (CMS), or Learning Management Systems (LMS).*

Net Generation – Children born between roughly 1980 and 1994.

OPAC (Online Public Access Catalog) – or (aka **iPAC** for Internet/Intranet Public Access Catalogue) is a computerized online catalog of the materials held in a library, or library system.

OpenOffice (OpenOffice.org) - An office suite application available for a number of different computer operating systems.

OpenSource - Means the source code is available to the users that harness the power of distributed peer review and transparency of process.

Orientation Island - First stop where Second Life newbies can learn the basics.

Permalink - A URL that points to a specific blogging entry even after the entry has passed from the front page into the blog archives. Because a permalink remains unchanged indefinitely, it is less susceptible to link rot.

Photo sharing - The publishing or transfer of a user's digital photos online, thus enabling the user to share them with others (whether publicly or privately).

Photoblog - A form of photo sharing and publishing in the format of a blog, but differentiated by the predominant use of and focus on photographs rather than text. Photoblogging is the action of posting photos to a photoblog, especially with advent of the moblog and cameraphones.

Photocasting – A way of sharing photos in which the pictures on the receivers computer automatically changes when you update it on yours.

Photostream - A looping slideshow of pictures posted to Flickr.

Podcast - A collection of digital media files which is distributed over the Internet using syndication feeds for playback on portable media players and personal computers. The term is a combination of the words *iPod* and *broadcast*.

Podcatcher - The colloquial name for a *web aggregator*. A Podcatcher provides technology that allows you to subscribe to podcasts.

Quality Slider - Most compression formats provide a slider controlling general video quality, measured in percentage.

Really Simple Syndication (RSS) - The de facto standard for the *syndication of Web content*. RSS is an XML-based format is in distributing news headlines on the Web.

Resident -Those with an active presence in Second Life.

Rich Internet Application (RIA) - Web-based applications that function as traditional desktop applications however Web browsers (or clients) are required for access but unlike traditional applications, software installation is not required, however depending on the application you usually will need to have Flash, ActiveX, Java, or similar technologies installed on the client machine.

RSS Aggregator - Also known as a feed reader, news reader or simply as an aggregator. A client software or a Web application which aggregates syndicated web content such as news headlines, blogs, podcasts, and vodcasts in a single location for easy viewing.

RSS Feed –An acronym for Real Simple Syndication or Rich Site Summary, a family of Web feed formats, specified in XML format used for syndicating Web content.

RSS Generator - Create RSS/XML feed files.

RSS Reader - A program to read RSS and Atom news feeds. Collect news in the background at user configurable intervals and alters when there is a new message.

Run-Down – Second-by-second breakdown of a TV or video show.

Screencast - A digital recording of computer screen output, also known as a *video screen capture*, often containing audio narration.

Service-oriented architectures (SOA) – IT infrastructure that allows different applications to exchange data and participate in business processes loosely coupled from the operating systems and programming languages underlying those applications.

Shelfari - A social cataloging Web site, where members can catalog, tag, review, and discuss books.

Signal noise - Noise between the microphone and the recording device.

Sims – A large plot of *Second Life* land that normally costs a minimum of $1,000.

SKYPE - A proprietary peer-to-peer Internet telephony (VoIP) network.

SkypeOut – Allows Skype users to call traditional telephone numbers, including mobile telephones, for a fee.

Social annotation - Social annotation, sometimes called web annotation, is software that allows users to "leave" comments on Web pages they visit, so that others visiting the page, and using the same software, can see their comments.

Social bookmarking - Social bookmarking is a method for Internet users to store, organize, search, and manage bookmarks of Web pages on the Internet with the help of metadata.

Social cataloging - A web application designed to help users catalog things--books, CDs, etc--owned or otherwise of interest to them.

Social networking - Focuses on the building and verifying of online social networks for communities of people who share interests and activities, or who are interested in exploring the interests and activities of others.

Social Constructionist Pedagogy - philosophy of learning that focuses on collaboration, activities and critical reflection.

Syndicate (Web syndication) - Making web feeds available from a site (publishing) in order to provide other people with a summary of the Web site's recently added content.

Tag - A keyword or term associated with or assigned to a piece of information.

Tag Cloud - A visual depiction of user-generated tags. The tags are usually hyperlinks that lead to a collection of items that are associated with a tag.

Teleport (or TP) - How avatars move instantly from spot to spot in the Virtual World of Second Life.

Thingamabrarians - Users of LibraryThing where they can catalog personal collections, keep reading lists, and meet other users who have the same books.

Tweets – Texted-based posts in Twitter.

Twitter - Twitter is a free social networking and micro-blogging service that allows users to send *updates* to the Twitter Web site, via short message service, instant messaging, or a third-party application.

V-commerce - Doing business in virtual worlds.

V-product -What you buy or sell in virtual worlds.

Virtual Learning Environments (VLE) - A software system designed to help teachers by facilitating the management of educational courses for their students, especially by helping teachers and learners with course administration.

Virtual Office - An environment that enables users to access, develop, and share documents online as opposed to on their desktop.

Vodcast – A video podcast is an online delivery of video on demand video clip content via Atom or RSS enclosures.

Web 2.0 - Refers to a perceived second generation of web-based communities and hosted services — such as social-networking sites, wikis, and folksonomies — that aim to facilitate creativity, collaboration, and sharing between users.

Widget - A portable chunk of code that can be installed and executed within any separate HTML-based Web page by an end user without requiring additional compilation.

Wiki - A software that allows users to easily create, edit, and link Web pages. Wikis are often used to create collaborative Web sites and to power community Web sites.

Wikibooks - Previously called Wikimedia Free Textbook Project and Wikimedia-Textbooks, is a Wikimedia Foundation wiki for the creation of free content textbooks and manuals.

Wikifarms – A server farm that provides wiki hosting, or a group of wikis hosted on such servers.

Wikinomics - Based on the book *Wikinomics: How Mass Collaboration Changes Everything* is by Don Tapscott and Anthony D. Williams that explores how some companies in the early 21st century have used mass collaboration (also called peer production) and open-source technology such as wikis to be successful.

Wikipedia - A multilingual, open content, free encyclopedia project operated by the non-profit Wikimedia Foundation.

Wikisource - The Free Library — is a Wikimedia project to build a free, wiki library of source texts, along with translations into any language and other supporting materials.

Wikiversity - A Wikimedia Foundation project, which supports learning communities, ad hoc teams, their learning materials, and resulting activities.

WYSIWYG - What You See Is What Your Get.

XML - The Extensible Markup Language (XML) is a general-purpose markup language that allows its users to define their own elements to facilitate the sharing of structured data across different information systems, particularly via the Internet.

Z39.50 - 9A client server protocol for searching and retrieving information from remote computer databases. It is widely used in library environments and is often incorporated into integrated library systems and personal bibliographic reference software.